THE VANISHING RIGHTS
OF THE STATES

JAMES M. BECK, LL.D.

THE VANISHING RIGHTS
OF THE STATES

A DISCUSSION OF THE RIGHT OF THE SENATE TO NULLIFY THE ACTION OF A SOVEREIGN STATE IN THE SELECTION OF ITS REPRESENTATIVES IN THE SENATE

BY

JAMES M. BECK, LL.D.

FORMER SOLICITOR GENERAL OF THE UNITED STATES
AUTHOR OF "THE CONSTITUTION OF THE UNITED STATES"

"Remove not the ancient Landmark, which thy fathers have set."
PROVERBS, XXII-28

NEW YORK
GEORGE H. DORAN COMPANY

TO

my grandson

JAMES MARSHALL TUCK

*whose middle name evidences his
proud heritage as a kinsman of
the greatest Interpreter
of the Constitution*
JOHN MARSHALL

INTRODUCTION

This monograph is not a lawyer's brief.

Its subject rises above the interests of any individual or party.

Its purpose is to challenge the attention of thoughtful men to a very serious question in constitutional law, with which both the Senate of the United States and the American people will soon be confronted. It has been written as a labor of love by one, who for many years in public addresses and books has endeavored to serve his day and generation by defending the Constitution of the United States against its critics and enemies.

Before committing this book to the press and submitting it to the consideration of that limited number of Americans who are seriously interested in constitutional problems, I wish to acknowledge the great assistance in this self-imposed labor of my friend, O. R. McGuire, a member of the Bar of Virginia and the District of Columbia. With his fine enthusiasm in the matter of historical research, he has exhaustively examined the records and precedents of the Senate and has accumulated a wealth of material which he has generously placed at my disposal.

If this book shall render any public service—as I hope it will—he is justly entitled to his share of the credit.

James M. Beck.

Washington, D. C.
November, 1926.

CONTENTS

APPENDICES

THE VANISHING RIGHTS
OF THE STATES

THE VANISHING RIGHTS OF THE STATES

CHAPTER I

THE EROSION OF THE CONSTITUTION

THE struggle to maintain the Constitution of the United States is an unending one.

The battle is always on, although the fact be little appreciated. The old saying "eternal vigilance is the price of liberty" is more than a meaningless platitude.

To the superficial observer, it would seem that the Constitution was never more strongly entrenched in the affections of the American people. In a sense, this is true. If the Constitution were submitted to-morrow as an entirety to a referendum, it would be re-adopted by a majority so preponderating as to approach unanimity.

This would not be due to any widespread knowledge on the part of the people of their Constitution, its historic background, or its essential political philosophy, but rather to the fact that the word "Constitution" conveys to the citizens the consciousness of the organic unity of the constituent states, and few, if any, question the immeasurable benefits which have resulted from the "Union," a name applied to the American commonwealth long before its present form.

The real danger to the Constitution lies in the gradual erosion of its principles, as from time to time, in the excesses of party strife, some one of these principles is so ignored that it ceases to be of vital force.

Washington recognized this in his Farewell Address when he prophesied that our form of Government would be much more easily "undermined" from within than overthrown by outward attack.

To the thoughtful American, the Constitution is not unlike the sandy beach on an ocean front. The encroaching waves each day ebb and flow. At high tide there is less beach and at low tide more. At times the beach will be devoured by the ocean, when a tempest has lashed it into a fury, and then the waters will become as placid as a mountain lake, and the shore will seem to have triumphed in this age-old struggle between land and water.

The owner of the upland is often deceived by the belief that the fluctuations of the battle generally leave the shore line intact, but when he considers the results of years, and not of months, he will realize that the shore has gradually lost in the struggle, and that slowly, but steadily, the ocean is eating into the land.

This is true of the erosion of our form of Government. Unhappily a written form of government is not a Gibraltar that can resist the waves, but a sandy beach, which, while it seems to beat back the devouring waters, is always losing in the struggle. Each decade sees some principle of the Constitution either weakened or nullified, and the difficulty is that the people are only sensible of their peril after the principle is destroyed, and when it is too late to restore it.

In this monograph the author wishes to illustrate this by a pending political controversy. He has selected a current incident in our political history which, at the moment, is very much in the minds of the people, and it is his purpose to show that now, as on many previous occasions, the constitutional aspects of the question are being subordinated, if not wholly lost sight of, in the controversy.

The theme of this monograph is thus less extensive than its broader title, to which many volumes could be devoted. My present purpose is an appeal to those, who still believe in the Constitution, to consider the limit of the powers of the Senate in determining the qualifications of its members.

The theme is not one of academic interest only. It has a very practical interest. It is likely, within a short time, to be the subject of vigorous, and possibly passionate, discussion on the floor of the Senate, and at the forum of public opinion. Any contribution to such a controversy, which involves a constitutional principle of vital importance, cannot be a wasted effort.

The circumstances out of which the present crisis grows are as follows:

In the spring of the current year, the States of Pennsylvania and Illinois held primaries to enable the voters of each of the two great historic parties of America to select their candidates for the Senate. These primaries were held under the laws of the States respectively. The votes which were cast were counted in the manner prescribed by the laws of such States. Under the methods of procedure, which both States provided, it was duly ascertained that William S. Vare had been chosen by the Republican electors of Pennsylvania to be the candidate of that party to the Senate, and that Frank L. Smith had been similarly chosen by the Republican electors of Illinois.

The principal contestants for the honor in each State acquiesced in the result, and no dispute has ever arisen that either of these gentlemen was not nominated. It appeared shortly thereafter that in both States large sums of money had been spent, not only for the successful, but for the unsuccessful candidates. While it is of no importance, so far as the constitutional question is concerned, it was clear that in each State the friends of the losing candidate had spent far more in his behalf than the friends of the successful candidate. Thus, in Pennsylvania, for every dollar that was spent by the friends of Mr. Vare, at least three dollars had been spent by his nearest opponent. The aggregate amounts, spent for both the successful and unsuccessful candidates, were possibly without any precedent in the history of primary elections, but neither Pennsylvania nor Illinois had ever imposed in their election laws any limit upon the amount of such expenditures. Presumably both States were of opinion that the real question, as affecting the regularity of a primary election, was not how much was spent, but the manner of its collection, and even more important, the manner of its disbursement.

It was not unnatural that the people of the United States

became interested in these bitterly contested primary elections and the Senate of the United States appointed a Committee to investigate both primaries.

I do not question the power of the Reed Committee to make the investigation nor the high motives which prompted its members to pursue their investigations. It was unquestionably developed that very large sums had been collected and disbursed, and in both cases the expenditure of some portions of the money was shown to be open to fair question, although no clear or tangible evidence was shown in this *ex parte* investigation that any sums had been corruptly disbursed and no evidence whatever that either candidate participated in any illegitimate expenditures.

In both States two things are clear.

The first is that the largest amount of money was expended for the legitimate, and indeed laudable, purpose of educating the voter upon the issues involved in these primary contests.

The second probable conclusion is that, if no moneys had been spent by the successful and unsuccessful candidates, the result would not have been different.

It is to be further noted that, in the absence of any law, which forbade the expenditure of money beyond a certain limit, each of the successful candidates was within his rights under the laws of his State in spending an unlimited amount of money, provided always that he collected it in a proper way and disbursed it for legitimate purposes. When Mr. Vare elected to test the sentiment of the Pennsylvania voters upon the vexed question of prohibition, he knew that he was opposed to a faction which could command almost unlimited resources. It was his undoubted right to seek a nomination for the Senate, and if he believed that the friends of his opponent would spend nearly $3,000,000, it was clearly within his right under the laws of Pennsylvania to spend one-third of that amount, always assuming that the expenditures were for the legitimate, and I emphasize, laudable purpose of educating the voters upon the merits of the issues which were involved.

A further significant fact is to be noted. The press gave, and properly, widespread publicity to the results of this legislative inquiry. It cannot be said that when the voters of Pennsylvania went to the polls in November, they were ignorant of the fact that a considerable sum of money had been spent by the friends of Mr. Vare to secure his nomination on the Republican ticket.

With full knowledge of the results of the inquiry, the people of Pennsylvania elected Mr. Vare to the Senate, and Illinois similarly selected Mr. Smith.

The sole question, therefore, is whether these States had the right to make such selections, or whether the Senate of the United States has the right to sit in judgment upon their deliberate choice.

When the Seventieth Congress convenes and proceeds to organize, it will thus be confronted with a problem of vital importance to our constitutional form of Government. Few questions could be more far-reaching.

It is reasonably certain that, when the Senate proceeds to organize, the senior Senator from Pennsylvania will present the credentials of the Honorable William S. Vare, as Senator-elect from Pennsylvania. The credentials will be in due form, and will certify by the signature of the Governor of Pennsylvania, and attested by the Great Seal of the State, that at a general election, held on November 2nd, 1926, the people of Pennsylvania, by a largely preponderating majority, elected Mr. Vare to the Senate of the United States. It is not probable that any question will be raised as to the regularity of the election, and it will not be doubted that the people of Pennsylvania did select Mr. Vare as one of its two representatives in the Senate of the United States. The candidate, who opposed Mr. Vare for this great office in the general election, will not only make no claim that he was elected, but will not himself contest the fact of such election.* It will not be questioned that Mr. Vare possesses all the qualifications for a Senator prescribed in the Constitution. It will be conceded that he has the requisite age, has been a citizen of the United States for the required period, and is an inhabitant of the State of Pennsylvania.

* See Appendix "C," p. 125.

Notwithstanding these conceded facts, it is now intimated by well-informed men, and even announced by some members of the Senate, who probably have not examined the testimony and who will be hereafter called upon to act judicially in the matter, that Mr. Vare's and Mr. Smith's credentials will be rejected, and that they will be denied their seats in the Senate.

Others high in authority, including also members of the Senate, have announced that while their credentials will be accepted, in accordance with the unbroken precedents of the Senate, they will be expelled, after they have been seated. Should this come to pass—and the author of this brochure refuses to believe it—it will unquestionably nullify the deliberate action of two sovereign States, in a matter which under the Constitution is within their reserved powers.

The interest which prompted this book is largely due to the inevitable effect which a *coup d'état* of this character might have upon the future of our institutions. Indeed, it suggests an inquiry of profound import, as to whether even our written form of Government can lastingly restrain the excesses of party strife.

It was a Tammany Congressman who once jocosely asked a great and noble democratic President—"what is the Constitution between friends?" The historic anecdote failed to tell us what Grover Cleveland's reply was. He was a Democrat of the old school, and believed that no party advantage could possibly justify an invasion of the Constitution. The joke became historic, and it was not as silly as it seemed.

If the experience of history teaches anything, it is the inability, for any great period of time, to restrain the living generation within the limitations of a Constitution, whether written or unwritten. Sooner or later the living generation refuses to be shackled by the mandates of the dead. The Constitution itself recognized this possibility and provided an orderly and deliberate method of amendment.

While the Constitution may, and generally does, survive "between friends," a more serious danger is presented, when the question arises as to the strength of its guarantees between political friends and enemies. In the noble Farewell Address, Washington, in expressing the counsels of an "old and affectionate friend" to future generations of America, expressed his great concern as to the effect of party Government upon the maintenance of the Constitution. He was sagacious enough to see that, when two political factions, each stimulated by great and powerful interests, and at times excited by passionate hatreds, were in conflict, there was manifest danger that each would forget "the rules of the game," as prescribed by the Constitution. He vainly cherished the hope that party Government might be avoided.

If men of this generation are under the illusion that a written form of Government can lastingly prevent acts of political parties, which are in violation of its principles, the men who framed the Constitution suffered from no such illusion. They had little faith that the Constitution could be more than a temporary bridge to span the gulf of social disorders which then prevailed. Their general feeling of doubt as to any permanent results from their labors was well expressed by one of their number (Mr. Gorham of Massachusetts), who, towards the close of the Convention, said he did not imagine that any member optimistically cherished the hope that the Constitution would last one hundred and fifty years. It has now lasted in form for one hundred and thirty-nine years, but its substance has been profoundly affected by the successive waves of party feeling, which have marked our history. The serious question in their minds was whether the American people would have sufficient self-restraint to maintain the Constitution in its integrity. They recognized that this would depend upon the question whether future generations of America would be—to use a modern philosophical term—pragmatists or moralists. If the spirit of pragmatism should be the greater influence, then the framers of the Constitution had little faith that their great work would be more than temporary.

The pragmatist judges everything from its immediate practical results, and that generally means the results upon his individual interests, or those of his party. The moralist, on the other hand, is little concerned with these practical consequences. To him the great question is the fundamental principle that is generally involved in every great conflict of political parties.

The framers of the Constitution were moralists. Long before the Revolution, the philosophical mind of Edmund Burke recognized this fact. Speaking of the good people of the Colonies, he said:

> "In other countries the people more simple and of less mercurial cast, judge of an ill principle in Government only by an actual grievance; here they anticipate evil, and judge of the pressure of the grievance by the badness of the principle."

A striking vindication of this sage observation of the greatest political philosopher of our English-speaking race was soon shown in the constitutional struggle, which culminated in our independence. If the Americans of the colonial period had been pragmatists, they would not have made so resolute an opposition to the enforcement of the stamp tax. They would have argued and—viewed pragmatically with reason,—that by this payment of a few million pounds, they were given in their state of infancy the protection of the greatest Empire which then existed. Fortunately for the future of America the men of the Revolution were not pragmatists, but moralists. They recognized that the power to tax was the power to destroy, and if the Colonists could be subjected to such taxations by an Act of Parliament, and without the consent of the colonial legislatures, they would be in a state of vassalage. To them the practical effects of the tax were as nothing in comparison with the great constitutional principle that "taxation without representation is tyranny."

The Constitution, as framed by the great Convention and reluctantly and grudgingly ratified by the American people, was the wisest and noblest assertion of constitutional morality in the annals of statecraft.

If the Fathers were dubious as to the future of that Constitution, it was not that they questioned its wisdom so much as they doubted the willingness of successive generations of Americans to accept its wise restraints.

Washington, writing to his friend and comrade in arms, the Marquis de Lafayette (then in France) on February 7, 1788, told him of the difficulties and complexities of the great Convention. Washington had at first been very reserved as to the merits of the compact, but, as the months passed on which followed its completion, he increasingly recognized that the result had been more sagacious and beneficent than he had anticipated. After stating that the powers of government had been very wisely distributed so as to prevent any undue concentration of power in any one man or body of men, he significantly added that the new government would be in no danger of degenerating into a monarchy, oligarchy or aristocracy, or any other form of despotism, "so long as there shall remain any virtue in the body of the people." He then continued:

> "I would not be understood, my dear Marquis, to speak of consequences which may be produced in the revolution of ages by corruption of morals, profligacy of manners, or *listlessness in the preservation of the natural and unalienable rights of mankind,* nor of the successful usurpations, that may be established at such an unpropitious juncture upon the ruins of liberty, however providently guarded and secured; as these are contingencies against which no human prudence can effectually provide."

Similarly Franklin—when, as it is said, with tears in his eyes he implored the delegates to sign the compact—uttered the same truth, for he said, in answer to those who saw fatal objections in the Constitution:

> "There is no form of government but what may be a blessing to the people if well administered for a course of years, and can only end in despotism, as other forms have done before it, when the people shall become so corrupted as to need despotic government, being incapable of any other."

In these utterances, Washington and Franklin were simply repeating, in different form, the warning of an earlier statesman of our colonial era, and one of the noblest founders of a state, William Penn, who expressed the truth by an analogy so simple that the humblest mind can grasp it. Penn said:

"Governments, like clocks, go from the motion men give them; and as governments are made and moved by men, so by them they are ruined, too. Therefore, governments depend upon men rather than men upon governments."

This great truth has been increasingly lost sight of by successive generations of Americans. Blinded by material prosperity, they are too apt to attach importance to the form of government and too little to the spirit of the people. It is not that the American people overvalue their Constitution, but that they grossly undervalue the part which they must play, if the Constitution is to endure.

The Constitution, as a scheme of government, speedily vindicated itself as it became the organic expression of our national unity and as it brought unbounded blessings to the millions of Americans that have come and gone. The Constitution has so far become a matter of common and beneficent experience that we are hardly conscious of its blessings, even as men little appreciate the blessing of breathing until some injury comes to the respiratory organs.

When we speculate as to the permanency of the Constitution, it is well to recall the teaching of the greatest master of political and natural science in the ancient world, a man who, even as late as the sixteenth century, was still the final word of wisdom in intricate problems. In his work on Politics, Aristotle said that no government could long endure unless it corresponded to the *"ethos"* of the people. He meant the aggregate of the habits, concepts, ideas, principles, and tendencies of a people, which give it its distinguishing character.

Undoubtedly, the Constitution, by upholding certain ideals of government, has itself a profound influence upon the spirit of the people, but it is also true that the spirit of the people necessarily has a profound influence upon the interpretation of the Constitution.   The *ethos* of a people may not be the spirit of their Constitution; and, in that event, it is not the spirit of the people which is destroyed, but the Constitution.*

* The author, in his recent book, "The Constitution of the United States," briefly dwells upon the many changes, to which the Constitution has been subjected in the ceaseless conflict between the obligation of the written word and the fleeting passions and insistent demands of living generations.   He said:

"Nevertheless, American history has shown that Macaulay was right in his underlying suggestion that no written document could wholly restrain the excesses of democracy.   Possibly the Constitution has proved more of a rudder than an anchor; for no state of human society is wholly static, and the Constitution guides, rather than holds.

The Constitution has been profoundly modified by public opinion,— which is more truly the organ of democracy than the ballot box.   As a result, many of its essential principles have been, as Washington warningly predicted, insidiously subverted, and many others are to-day threatened by direct attack.

Thus, the basic principle of home rule has been, to some extent, subverted by the submergence of the States.

Property rights, as guaranteed by the Fifth and Fourteenth Amendments, have been impaired by many socialistic measures.   The difficulty has not been in the principles of constitutional law; but in their application to complex facts, and the ascertainment of those facts has put an impossible burden upon the Judiciary.

The system of governmental checks and balances has been destroyed by the persistent subordination, in the practical workings of the Government, of the Legislature to the Executive.

The commercial power of the Union has been utilized to attain unconstitutional ends, to the substantial destruction of the rights of the States.

The Fifteenth Amendment is, in many States, a dead letter.

The concurrent power of the Senate in the selection of diplomatic representatives and in the making of treaties has frequently been impaired by protocols, informal treaties, and other executive acts, which make a free decision of the Senate difficult, if not impossible.

Above all, the taxing system has been perverted since the Sixteenth Amendment to redistribute property. . . .

No student of our institutions can question that the Constitution is in graver danger today than at any other time in the history of America.   This is due, not to any conscious hostility to the spirit or letter, but to the indifference and apathy with which the masses regard the increasing assaults upon its basic principles.

Unless the American people awaken to the necessity of defending their most priceless heritage, there is manifest danger that within the lives of those now living the form will survive the substance of the faith.

The thoughtful few, who from time to time sound this warning, are "as one crying in the wilderness."   Their voices are lost in the roar of a mechanical civilization.   Of the few, who seem to care, many are fatalists, who having filled their own granaries with material abundance, complacently say with Louis XV, "after me, the deluge."

Beck's *Constitution of the United States,* pp. 271-3.

Nothing at the present time more strikingly illustrates this change in the *ethos* of the people than the apparent indifference of the American people to the threat that the Senate of the United States will nullify the deliberate decisions of the great States of Pennsylvania and Illinois. The spirit of pragmatism is shown by the fact that, while the merits of the primary campaigns are much discussed and opinions are divided as to whether, even in those populous States, the large sums of money could be properly spent, yet little consideration is given to the fundamental question whether the Constitution gives to the Senate any power to sit in judgment upon the decision of the sovereign States, especially in a matter so vital· to them as the choice of their representatives in the Senate. It seems to be generally assumed, and was assumed in the resolution offered by Senator La Follette in the closing days of the last session of Congress, that the Senate has absolute power to expel any member whom it thinks unworthy of membership in that body, even though the people of the State, which accredited the member as its representative, are of a different opinion.

If this be so, the sovereign States do not themselves select their representatives in the Senate. They merely *nominate* them, and the ultimate judge of the moral and political qualifications of the accredited senator is the Senate itself. This was the very method of selecting Senators which the Constitutional Convention rejected, as will by hereafter shown. (See Chapter III.)

Thus no doctrine would have surprised the framers of the Constitution more than this assumption. Indeed, it is safe to say that the Constitution of the United States would never have been adopted if its framers had conceived as a possibility any such power in the Senate. *If such a power shall be recognized, then the greatest of the rights of the States will have vanished.*

The Senate was created by the Constitution to preserve the rights and prestige of the States. The members of the House of Representatives more truly represented the new force which was then coming into existence, namely, the peoples of the

States. The Senate, however, was intended to represent the States as political entities. In it each was to be represented on a plane of absolute and indestructible equality. To preserve the rights of the States, great and exceptional powers were given to the Senate. No law could be passed without the concurrence of the Senate. No important appointment to public office could be made without its consent. No treaty could have any efficacy unless two-thirds of the Senate concurred. No war could be declared unless the Senate so voted.

All these considerations made, and were intended to make, the Senate the last rampart of the power of the States. Under the primitive conditions of those simple days, the Fathers did not and could not appreciate, that a complex industrial age was about to dawn, when, with the centripetal influence of steam and electricity, the consolidation of the Union and the submergence of the States into a central Government would proceed with accelerating speed. While they vaguely feared the ultimate outcome, they little realized that within less than a century and a half—the period which Mr. Gorham marked as the maximum duration of the Constitution—the States would lose many of their powers and would become, for many practical purposes, and certainly in the imagination of the American people, little more than subordinate police provinces. While it is true that Alexander Hamilton suggested this as a desirable form of Government, he had, as one of his fellow delegates said, "few admirers and no supporters." Nevertheless, in many respects, the rejected project of Alexander Hamilton has become the reality of to-day.

The power of the States—without which the Constitution would never have been either framed or ratified—is not wholly gone, and will not be destroyed as long as the Senate exists to represent peculiarly the States as States. It is not likely that the powers of the Senate will ever be destroyed by any amendment to the Constitution. These powers are the great bulwarks of the Constitution and protect the Republic from that fate which has marked the end of other nations, namely, the undue concentration of power in one man or magistrate. The Senate is the great conservative force of the political department of the Government, and one can say of it, as Byron said of the Coliseum, that while it stands, Rome will stand.

In vain, however, the preservation of the powers of the Senate, if the final choice of Senators is no longer the free act of the States, but becomes a matter for the final decision of the Senate. Should this principle become a part of our constitutional form of Government, then the membership of the Senate will be whatever a majority of the Senate desires it to be.

If such a principle were once permanently established, the selection of Senators would not be the action of the States, —except primarily—and the final selection would be by a majority of the Senate. *If sixty-four senators can unseat two senators by expulsion, they could unseat thirty-two. Even forty-nine senators could refuse to receive the credentials of forty-seven. Thus a coup d'état is at any time possible.*

While the author prefers to discuss this matter independently of any existing party divisions, he cannot refrain from expressing his surprise that distinguished members of the Democratic Party, whose historic policy has been that of States' rights, should have expressed themselves as in favor of a course of action, which would be the destruction of the most vital and basic of these rights.

Imagine, for sake of argument, a recrudescence of that baneful spirit of sectionalism, which once unhappily divided the American people; that the line of division between the two great historic parties should again become geographical and run along the Mason and Dixon's Line. Such a supposition is improbable, and no true American would wish to regard it as a possibility. If such possibility were one day realized, and a Republican majority in the Senate desired to strengthen their control by refusing to seat newly elected domocratic Senators, might they not do so on the pretext, if the Senate has the powers now claimed for it, that the Senators-elect had not been selected by a free and fair vote, or might not a Republican majority provide that, unless a majority of the qualified electors actually voted, it should be presumed that they had not been permitted to vote and that there was, therefore, no true election?

Thoughtful men of all sections would deprecate any such recrudescence of the sectional question, for their attitude towards the question of white supremacy in the South is not unsympathetic. But such an inference from the failure of a portion of the electorate to vote is no more unreasonable than the assumption that because large sums of money have been spent in a heated primary campaign in great and populous States like Pennsylvania and Illinois, such sums were either corruptly collected or corruptly disbursed.

It is not, however, important whether the inference in either case is or is not justified. The all important consideration is that under the Constitution the States reserved to themselves, and the peoples thereof, the right to select their own representatives in the Senate. While the right of the Senate to determine whether an individual, who claims to be thus elected, has actually been elected at the general election is clear, and while it also has the right to determine, whether the men who have been selected as Senators by the States actually possess the qualifications prescribed in the Constitution, yet the right of the Senate to sit in judgment upon the action of sovereign States goes no further.

Whether a federal law could or should be passed that arbitrarily fixes the amount of money to be spent in a primary election is another and very difficult problem. It takes no account of the difference in population in different States. It takes even less account of the fact that in some elections very little money can be legitimately spent, and that in other, and bitterly contested elections, where great questions of public policy are involved, large sums of money can be legitimately spent to educate the voter.

The apathy or ignorance of the voter is more to be feared than the corruption of the voter. In the last fifty years we have witnessed an alarming and portentous loss of interest by the average citizen in the selection of public officers. In the Tilden-Hayes campaign, over 82% of the qualified electorate voted, and in recent elections, when a President was selected, only 48% voted. It is impossible to induce the average citizen to vote unless he becomes interested, and it is equally impossible to induce him to make a wise choice unless he be educated as to the comparative merits of the candidates, or the importance of the questions of policy which are involved.

The legitimate expenditure of money to interest and educate voters serves a great public purpose. In populous States like Pennsylvania and Illinois, especially in a bitterly contested campaign, this requires a considerable expenditure of money. Pennsylvania has a population of nearly 10,000,000. To reach nearly two million voters by printed literature, press advertisements and public meetings requires a considerable expenditure of money. To say arbitrarily that the expenditure of a given amount is necessarily illegal, is to adopt a ruling which has no justification either in morals or in the experience of mankind.* As Doctor Johnson once said: "Let us avoid cant," and the author adds, hypocrisy. Thus, if the sum were arbitrarily fixed at $25,000 in each State, it would be a gross injustice to say that the 10,000,000 citizens of New York could spend no more in their election than the citizens of smaller states, less in population than the inhabitants of a single ward in one of New York's populous cities.

We are, however, only now concerned with the fundamental question of the power to nullify the action of a Sovereign State. It goes to the very foundation of constitutional government.

Before proceeding to quote and discuss the pertinent provisions of the Constitution, it will be well to recall a great and noble fight for popular government, which took place in the mother country about two decades before the Constitutional Convention, and which the framers of the Constitution had in mind when they defined the powers of the Senate to expel a member.

I refer to the case of John Wilkes.

---

* Mr. Vare admitted a personal contribution to his nomination campaign of $71,000. This would not suffice to print and post one appeal to the entire qualified electorate of Pennsylvania.

CHAPTER II

NOTHING more strikingly illustrates the old maxim that "eternal vigilance is the price of liberty" than the fact that the battles of constitutional liberty must be fought over again by each succeeding generation. Thus the supremacy of the people in Parliament proved a long struggle of many centuries and with varying fortunes. The tide of battle ebbed and flowed, now in favor of the absolutism of the Crown, and later, the supremacy of the people.

Few chapters in English history are more noteworthy than the valorous battle which Eliott, Hampden and Pym fought to maintain the principle that the Crown could not impose taxes upon the people without the consent of their representatives in Parliament. That struggle culminated in the reign of Charles the First, and cost that unhappy monarch his head.

The unceasing battle between absolutism and public liberty then took another form. If the Crown could not impose taxes without the consent of Parliament, then it became necessary to control Parliament itself. This great battle was fought and won for the cause of popular government a decade before the Declaration of Independence by a man who, although he did not possess as noble a personality as Eliott, Hampden or Pym, must, nevertheless, be regarded as one of the great heroes in the struggle for constitutional liberty. I refer to John Wilkes.

It is certain that the men who signed the Declaration of Independence, and subsequently adopted the Constitution of the United States, were profoundly influenced, not merely by the great controversy between Eliott, Hampden and Pym and Charles the First as to the right of taxation, but even more by the struggle of John Wilkes to vindicate the right of the

29

people of Middlesex to select their own representative in the House of Commons without interference either by a majority of the House or by the King himself. "Wilkes and Liberty" was the rallying cry of all lovers of freedom, not only in England but throughout the Colonies.

The embattled farmers who fired the shot that was "heard around the world" had been greatly influenced by John Wilkes, a fearless member of the English Parliament, who, single-handed, taught George III that English kings could no longer exclaim with Louis XIV, *"L'état, c'est moi."* He also taught the same King and his ministers the power of public opinion in maintaining the rights of English voters to be represented in Parliament by men of their choice.

John Wilkes was the son of an English tradesman. He became interested in public life through the influence of George Grenville when the two political parties of England were the Whigs and the Tories. The death of Henry Pelham had deprived the Whigs of a leader, who, for more than a decade, had been the leader of his party in Parliament. During more than forty years of uninterrupted reign of power, the Whigs had steadily maintained the "principles of the Revolution." These principles were the preservation of the supremacy of Parliament, as delineated in the Bill of Rights, and the maintenance of the Hanoverian succession, which had been defined by the Act of Settlement. Since the first two Georges troubled themselves little with the concerns of their English subjects and were unable to speak the English language, they were content with a limited monarchy and never challenged the authority of Parliament or the right of the electors to be represented by men of their own choice. George III, remembering the words of his mother, "George, be a King," had scarcely ascended the throne when he resolved to reduce Parliament to its impotence in the days of the Stuarts.

He began his assault on Parliament by joining hands with discontented factions of the Whigs and Tories to unseat Pitt, the great Commoner, as Prime Minister. This combination was successful in its object and Lord Bute, an incompetent favorite, was placed in power. Bute was soon at issue with the press and he established a ministerial organ, which was christened "The Briton," with Tobias Smollett as editor, to defend him. The opportunity of meeting the apologist of the Government in controversy was irresistible, and Wilkes lost no time in setting up, on June 5, 1762, a rival paper, which, in derision, he dubbed "The North Briton." Wilkes' paper was well written, terse and epigrammatic, and from the first proved a great success.

A change of ministerial offices now followed the removal of Pitt. George III found it necessary to purchase a majority of the House of Commons who would favor peace with France and Henry Fox, the paymaster, was selected for the purpose, replacing George Grenville as "Manager" of the lower House. A system of wholesale bribery and intimidation now took place which possibly was never surpassed in the history of Parliament. A host of superfluous bureaucrats was created, and innumerable political renegades were rewarded by rich sinecures. "A shop was publicly opened at the Pay Office," declared Horace Walpole, "where the members flocked and received the wages of their venality in bank bills." It was made plain to all that while the King's friends would be lavishly rewarded, his enemies would be ruthlessly proscribed.

As a public warning, George III struck the name of Pitt from the list of Privy Councillors with his own hand and the whole of the Civil Service was microscopically examined, the humblest clerk being discharged without explanation, if he was even suspected of being a supporter of the opposition. Every vote, both in Parliament and in the election districts, was regarded as the personal property of the King. At last, George III had seemingly had his way and the House of Commons lay impotent at his feet.

The triumph was short-lived. John Wilkes was still to be reckoned with, and few chapters in English history are nobler than his struggle against absolutism.

The press was not yet wholly silenced. The ministerial organ was no match for the "North Briton" and the vitriolic pen of John Wilkes. Bute was soon overwhelmed by a storm of obloquy and ridicule. He bowed before it and fled, seeking solace amongst his prints and flowers, haughty and aloof to most of mankind. George Grenville, who had been estranged from Lord Temple, his brother, ever since he had joined the Bute ministry, succeeded to the office of Prime Minister. The "North Briton" had failed to appear on the previous Saturday for the first time since its establishment, but at the opening of Parliament on April 19, 1763, the references in the King's Speech to the preliminary articles of peace induced Wilkes to enter the lists as a champion of liberty. As with the sonorous blast of a trumpet he published the famous "No. 45" of the "North Briton."

He laid down the proposition, which has long since been accepted as a truism, that the "King's Speech has always been considered by Parliament and by the Public at large as the Speech of the Minister." Thereupon he proceeded to criticize the speech. After protesting that the reference to the King of Prussia contained "an infamous fallacy," he asserted the "honor of the Crown" was "sunk even to prostitution."

This was "the straw that broke the camel's back." George III demanded that Wilkes be crushed. Grenville believed that he was in honor bound to make an example of his old friend and Lords Halifax and Egremont were burning to avenge, not only their King, but insults that had been heaped upon them. A general warrant of search and seizure, the same kind of an instrument which James Otis was boldly challenging in Boston, was issued and Wilkes and his printers were arrested. Wilkes pleaded his privilege from arrest as a member of Parliament and the invalidity of the general warrant. The Court held that his arrest was invalid, and as Wilkes left the court room he found himself in the midst of a multitude, ten thousand strong, every man of them his defender, shouting, "Wilkes and Liberty."

Foiled in his attempt to punish Wilkes through the courts and stung to the quick by the greatness of his popularity, George III gave orders to his servile followers that Wilkes must be expelled from Parliament. Before his release from arrest, Wilkes had imprudently reprinted the "North Briton" in volume form and had printed twelve copies for a few intimates of an obscene "Essay on Woman," a parody on Pope's "Essay on Man." These publications were made the pretext for his expulsion from the House of Commons.

Parliament met on November 15, 1763. For many weeks the whole nation had been looking forward to this day, as though a decisive battle was to be lost or won. All were aware that on the outcome of the issue between George III and Wilkes, as the champion of the People, depended the momentous question whether an English King or the electors should decide who should represent the people in the House of Commons. Long before the Speaker took his seat, every bench was filled in the House of Commons and members who could not obtain seats were standing around the walls. Dense crowds were gathered in the courtyards outside the old palace of Westminster and members of Parliament thronged the long corridors of the immense building. Each face was aglow with expectation; all hurried to and fro with quick, eager footsteps. It was one of the great moments in English history. Then the English-speaking people on both sides of the Atlantic had a militant sense of constitutional morality. They were willing to fight for their rights.

There sat in the House of Commons the great William Pitt, grim and aloof, his fiery eloquence for the moment stilled. There also sat Colonel Isaac Barré, who had fought with Wolfe on the Plains of Abraham, and the greatest orator in the House of Commons, except Pitt, Charles Townsend, and Edmund Burke. The King's Speech, delivered by George Grenville, requested the House of Commons to consider the case of John Wilkes, and Lord North followed with a motion, declaring the North Briton No. 45 "a false, scandalous and seditious libel." All through the long evening, Pitt retained the center of the stage, throwing his whole soul into the struggle, since he knew that the right of representation was at stake. Lord North, with the knowledge that three hundred members were at his command, was content to utter empty platitudes on the subject of sedition and treason. It was nearly two o'clock in the morning when the motion was put to a vote and carried by 273 to 111. The victory of the King was to be temporary, a Bull Run preceding an Appomattox.

Lord Sandwich, a greater rake than Wilkes, opened the fight against him in the House of Lords by reading passages from the "Essay on Woman," and had little difficulty in carrying a motion declaring that the Essay was a scandalous, obscene and impious libel. Probably the morals of most of the noble Lords were little better than those of Wilkes. It was not an age of Josephs. In those days Potiphar's wife would not lack suitors. Both Houses of Parliament ordered Wilkes to attend, but he had been wounded in a duel with a member of Parliament and had gone to Paris to recuperate. While he was in Paris, George III ordered his expulsion from the House of Commons and, on January 20, 1763, the motion was carried.

Thereafter, on February 15, 1763, Sir William Meredith opened a great debate in the House of Commons on the matter of general warrants, and the King found to his dismay that he was able to secure a majority of only ten votes, while the opposition had increased its total to the formidable number of 197. Never before in living memory had greater orators followed each other in Parliament in closer succession and never before had it been necessary for the King to mobilize his invalids— gouty old gentlemen wrapped in blankets, victims of rheumatism and influenza, muffled in shawls, being carried from their beds in the wintry London night to save their leaders from political destruction. "The floor of the House," said Horace Walpole, "looked like the pool of Bethesda."

Like Banquo's ghost, Wilkes would not down. Notwithstanding that he had been tried and convicted by the courts for libel and had been declared an outlaw, he quitted the Continent after a three-year sojourn and returned in 1767 to London to renew the battle. The freedom of the City was presented to him and a fund was raised to defray his expenses of reëlection, as well as to pay his private debts. In the colonies the interest in the struggle was intense. South Carolina contributed, through her legislature, the sum of 1500 pounds and in Pennsylvania, the citizens of Wyoming Valley named their infant city, Wilkes-Barre. He then announced his candidacy for a seat in Parliament.

Defeated in his first candidacy for one of the London seats, he immediately announced his candidacy for one of the two seats for the County of Middlesex. Soon after six o'clock on the eventful morning of the election, a stream of coaches, decked with blue favors and with passengers wearing blue cockades and carrying "Wilkes and Liberty" cards, set out for the polling places.

Wilkes was overwhelmingly elected and, as the voters returned through the West End of London, many houses were compelled to illuminate their windows in honor of the people's victory. Carriages in the street were marked with "No. 45" and all who would not shout "Wilkes and Liberty" were beaten and insulted. Some of the voters invaded Berkeley Square and broke the glass in Lord Bute's stately residence. The tumult continued for two days. Upon nearly every door in town was scrawled "No. 45." Few vehicles were allowed to pass the streets without that number. The Austrian Ambassador was dragged from his carriage and "No. 45" chalked upon the soles of his shoes. The city was illuminated. The people cared nothing for Wilkes' debts, his libertinage nor his blasphemy. It was enough for them that he should return to England as an outlaw and again take up their fight for liberty. His courage, like the mantle of charity, covered a multitude of sins.

While the Government had made no attempt to enforce either his conviction for libel or outlawry, Wilkes announced prior to his election that he would voluntarily appear before Lord Chief Justice Mansfield and, true to his announcement, he made his appearance. Lord Mansfield set aside the outlawry on a technical ground, but Judge Yates sentenced him to twenty-two months in prison for printing "North Briton No. 45" and the "Essay on Woman." He took up his residence in one of the most sumptuous suites of rooms in the prison at St. George's Fields, where he served his sentence. From his prison, he vigorously conducted his new campaign for reelection.

In the meantime, Parliament had met and George III declared that "the expulsion of Mr. Wilkes appears to be very essential and must be effected." Having overthrown Bute, made a laughing-stock of Grenville, sown discord amongst the adherents of Rockingham, and defeated the power of the Crown in his election from Middlesex, Wilkes was in the mood to take the initiative and carry his fight against expulsion into the House of Commons. A vacancy occurring in Middlesex, Wilkes secured the election, as his colleague, of Sergeant Glynn, who had so ably prosecuted his suits against the officers of the Crown for damages because of the general warrants and who had defended him in the prosecutions for libel. At once new proceedings were instituted to expel Wilkes. Determined to omit no pretext for his expulsion, the Attorney General was entrusted with a motion, declaring Wilkes guilty of an "insolent, scandalous libel" and, although Blackstone objected seriously that the matter was one for a judge and jury, the King had sufficient servile supporters in the House of Commons to carry the motion.

George III pressed relentlessly on. Upon the reassembling of Parliament the following Friday, Lord Barrington, the Secretary of War, moved for the expulsion of Wilkes. During the course of the debate, George Grenville, who, as Prime Minister, had been the victim of the vitriolic "North Briton No. 45," bravely declined to go the length proposed by the King and delivered a brilliant speech of remonstrance against the expulsion, and vindicated the right of the people of Middlesex to be represented in the House of Commons by a man of their own choice.* All honor to Grenville! He was brave enough in the teeth of powerful opposition—even of an almost absolute King—to defend with all the passion of his powerful intellect the right of representation—a right which he had dealt a heavy blow a few years before in leading the forces of George III in the first expulsion of Wilkes.

Edmund Burke, the friend of liberty everywhere, including the far-off colonies in America, raised his golden voice in support of Grenville, and demanded scornfully how the alleged

---

* Grenville's noble speech is given in full in Appendix "B," p. 94.

offense of libel could deprive Wilkes of his right of being elected into Parliament.

Protest was in vain. The motion to expel Wilkes was carried by a majority of 82 after a long debate, in which most, if not all, of the leading members of Parliament took part. From his prison in St. George's Fields, Wilkes assured his constituents that his courage was not affected and appealed to them to assert their right "of naming their own representatives" by reëlecting him to Parliament. He declared to his constituents:

> "If ministers can once usurp the power of declaring who *shall not* be your representative, the next step is very easy, and will follow speedily. It is that of telling you whom you *shall* send to Parliament, and then the boasted Constitution of England will be entirely torn up by the roots."

Change the word "ministers" to "Senators," "Parliament" to "Congress" and "England" to the "United States" and his words will fit as a glove the coming controversy in the Senate.

The rain fell in torrents on election day, but a great crowd assembled at the polling place. No candidate ventured to oppose Wilkes, and he was again elected "by the unanimous voice of above two thousand of the most respectable freeholders." Gentlemen on horseback, with drums beating, French horns playing, and colors flying, serenaded Wilkes in his prison, and felicitated him upon his reëlection.

The next day, the House of Commons, on motion of Lord Strange, resolved that "Wilkes was incapable of being elected a member to serve in the present Parliament." The undaunted Wilkes from his prison again announced his candidacy for the Borough of Middlesex.

Four weeks elapsed before the next election in Middlesex. It was not until the evening before the election that George III could induce a candidate to oppose Wilkes, but even then no one could be secured to nominate the King's candidate. Wilkes was unanimously reëlected for a third time. On the next day the House of Commons again declared the election to be null and void. Again Wilkes' only answer was to announce his candidacy for the vacant seat.

Before the next election, George III secured the profligate, Colonel Henry Lawes Luttrell, a man who had borne an unsavory renown from his school days, to oppose Wilkes. The temper of the people of England was raised to a fever pitch and the electors of Middlesex resolved that they would continue to reëlect Wilkes as often as a subservient House of Commons obeyed George III in expelling him. The country resounded with shouts of "Wilkes and no King," and it became evident that the English people were ready for open rebellion in defense of the freedom of election. The mere presentation of an address to the King by some of the merchants of London excited the populace to the wildest fury, and zealous loyalists, passing through the streets of London to St. James Palace, encountered riotous multitudes, who hurled insults at them and pelted them with sticks and stones.

Luttrell was believed to run such personal risks in the approaching election that odds were freely offered against his life and the authorities looked forward to election day with grave apprehension. A proclamation was issued and the streets were lined with soldiers under instructions to quell any disturbance, no matter what the cost. On the morning of election, cavalcades of horsemen, four abreast, waving banners and flags bearing the watchwords, "Magna Charta" and "Bill of Rights," preceded long lines of coaches decked in blue to the polling place. Many ladies wore breast-knots of blue and silver in honor of Wilkes and men wore blue cockades in his honor. It took the united efforts of such friends of Wilkes as James Townsend and Sergeant Glynn to protect Luttrell from the voters. The poll was closed at five o'clock. Wilkes had been again reëlected by a vote of 1143 to 296 for Luttrell. Again there was a parade through the streets of London and Wilkes was again serenaded in prison.

From across the Atlantic came greetings and encouragement to Wilkes from the American Colonists. They recognized that his cause was their cause. Wilkes was kept informed by

American newspapers and American correspondents of the enthusiasm for liberty and freedom of elections that his struggle had awakened in the breasts of the American colonists. His name became a popular toast. The Committee of the Sons of Liberty at Boston borrowed their name from an expression used by Colonel Barré in the House of Commons in opposition to the first expulsion of Wilkes and a communication was sent to him from the Committee, signed by John Adams, Joseph Warren, Benjamin Church, Thomas Young and Benjamin Kent, congratulating him on his success, while, as heretofore stated, the far-off colony of South Carolina sent him £1500 to aid him in paying his debts.

No event in England gave greater encouragement to the militant party in the American Colonies than the achievements of Wilkes and his health was drunk on every 14th of August by the Sons of Liberty in Boston, when they gathered around the Liberty Tree. In trying to vindicate the rights of the electorate against George III, he was fighting for a principle dear to the hearts of the colonists, and his numerous victories served to remind them that they "who would be free themselves must strike the blow." Had they not been inspired by his brave example, it is possible that they would not have dared to declare their independence.

The fourth return of Wilkes to Parliament goaded George III to greater lengths, and wholly unmindful of the fact that not only were the eyes of Englishmen throughout the world watching the outcome, but that the attention of Europe was fastened on the struggle, he gave orders to his followers to expel Wilkes again and that Luttrell be declared elected. His sycophants hastened to do his bidding, which was accomplished by a majority of 69 votes.

The end of the long struggle was at hand. The King and his party, while victorious in every attempt to expel Wilkes, had won only Pyrrhic victories. They now realized the impotence of their efforts. It was clear that the people of England were so aroused that they would continue to reëlect Wilkes to the House of Commons as long as a subservient majority of Royalists were pleased to unseat him. Nothing was left to the Royalist Party but to yield to the inevitable. Accordingly, a motion was made in Wilkes' behalf to expunge from the records of the House the resolutions of expulsion and the previous resolution of February 17, 1769, which had declared that he was incapable of being elected a member of the House of Commons.

The victory—after a prolonged struggle—had been won. Seemingly the right of a free people to select their own representatives would never again be called in question in an English-speaking nation—and yet, to-day the old question again confronts the free people of America in the one hundred and fiftieth year of American independence—God save the mark!

With the further career of Wilkes, this book is not concerned. It is enough to say that the people of London crowned their champion not merely with the honor of a seat in Parliament, but by electing him High Sheriff and later, Lord Mayor. While serving his terms as Lord Mayor, his office became the center of those who, either in England, France or America, were endeavoring to restore the rights of the people. It was this circumstance that made him so disliked by confirmed Tories, like Dr. Samuel Johnson, and the method by which the crafty Boswell brought the gruff old doctor and John Wilkes together at a dinner is familiar to all readers of Boswell's Johnson. While Wilkes was a profligate and somewhat of a blackguard, yet Johnson, despite all his antipathies, found him a very pleasant table companion.

Americans may also recall with interest that it was at the house of John Wilkes, when he was Lord Mayor, that Arthur Lee, of Virginia, shortly after the Battle of Lexington, met Beaumarchais, an adventurer of much the same type as John Wilkes. It was from Arthur Lee that Beaumarchais learned of the brave revolt of the Colonies and this prompted him to return to France and interest Louis XVI and Vergennes, the Foreign Minister, in secretly intervening for the Colonies. Thus, Washington's little army obtained the supplies of arms and ammunition, without which the War of Independence would have come to a disastrous conclusion within a few years from Lexington.

The Middlesex election was the great constitutional landmark of the Eighteenth Century. It determined for all time
the right of Englishmen to be represented in Parliament by
members of their own choice, for no King or Minister has
ever since dared to challenge that right. It also had far-reaching effect in parliamentary reform in England and what is
more important to Americans, it showed them the futility of
expecting liberty from the Government of George III. It
nerved them for the long struggle, which led through Brandy-
wine, Valley Forge and Yorktown to the Constitutional Convention of 1787, where the right of electors to be represented
by persons of their choice was, as it was thought, indestructibly
written into the charter of our Government.*

* Under these circumstances, is it not amazing that at this late day,
it can be gravely suggested by leaders of thought, and even by members
of the Senate, that if the Senate accepts the credentials of William S. Vare
they will then proceed to invoke the right of expulsion, in order to
nullify the will of the people of Pennsylvania? There is no essential
difference between the John Wilkes case and the William S. Vare case,
except that in the case of Wilkes, the fate of a scurrilous radical was
involved, who had offended the laws of England, and who was charged
with having traduced the ministers of the Crown by libelous pamphlets.
In the case of Mr. Vare, we have a citizen of Pennsylvania, who has
served for many years with credit in the House of Representatives, and
against whom there is no charge except that in a heated contest for a
primary nomination, he had expended in educating the voters the sum
of $71,000, and that a far larger sum had been spent in his behalf by his
friends. It is not charged that Mr. Vare violated any law of the State
of Pennsylvania or of the United States. If he did, he could be indicted,
and if found guilty, punished. In that event, he would have a fair trial
under the rules of law.
The expulsion of Vare, to please the clamorous minority who demand it,
would be a fatal backward step in our history. It would indubitably
show that the people of the United States in 1926 were not as capable of
constitutional government as were the people of England in 1769, when
against the power of the Crown and a corrupt majority of the House of
Commons, the brave electors of Middlesex successfully maintained their
right to select their own representative in Parliament.

CHAPTER III

THE Declaration of Independence severed the tie which had bound the Colonies to England. Thereupon, thirteen independent, proud and self-conscious States came into being. The period of the controversial years, which have been called the "critical period" of American history, taught them that they must create a Government for certain common purposes. To this great end, twelve of the thirteen States sent representatives to a Convention to frame a Constitution for a Union of the States.

Before that Convention met, rivalry between the large and the small States had developed. The great question in the Convention was whether or not all the States, large or small, should have an equal representation in the Senate. From May 25, 1787, until July 16, this great question was debated ably and so fiercely that, at one crisis, the smaller States threatened to secede.

To all the question was vital, because the Senate was to be given extraordinary powers in the new Government. Its members were to be the "elder statesmen" of the Republic. Their tenure of office was to be longer than either that of the members of the House or of the Chief Executive. No law could be enacted by the House without the concurrence of the Senate, and the President could not appoint any of the principal officers of the Government without such consent, and could not make a treaty unless two-thirds thereof concurred. With such extraordinary powers, the equality of representation in the Senate become a vital matter, and on July 16th a compromise was finally reached which recognized the equality of the Sovereign States, and the right of each of them to have two representatives of their own selection in the Senate. The importance of the Senate in the new Government is evidenced by the fact that, while all other parts of the Constitution are amendable, this portion alone is unchangeable.

Even more vital than the equality of membership was the manner of selection. The small States would have won a barren victory if they could not select their own Senators, or if, having selected them, a majority of the Senate could unseat them. If such majority were to be the final judge as to who was a fit member for each State in the Senate, then the rights of the States were of small account indeed.

In the first drafts of the Constitution it was proposed that the state legislatures should merely nominate eligible men for the Senate, and that the Federal House of Representatives should, from among these nominees, select the Senate. The futility of this plan, if the Sovereign States were to preserve their identity, was quickly recognized, and the Constitution, as finally ratified, provided that the Senators should be selected by the Legislatures of their States. While the Seventeenth Amendment changed the method of election, it reaffirmed the great principle that each State was its own judge as to the character of men that it would send as its representatives to this august and powerful body.

The members of the Constitutional Convention of 1787 comprised men of accurate and exact scholarship in the field of political study and research.

There were twenty-four resolutions agreed to in the Constitutional Convention expressive of the general plan of government. The 4th, 11th and 22nd related to the organization of the Senate. These general resolutions were referred to the Committee on Detail. When the Committee on Detail made its report, the Convention modified it in many particulars and the modifications were referred to a Committee on Style. The Convention also modified the report of the Committee on Style and, as thus modified, the resolutions were embodied in the Constitution.

The Virginia Plan, submitted by John Randolph, provided, in paragraph 5, for a second branch of the Legislature, to be called a Senate, to be elected by the lower House out of a suitable number nominated by the state legislatures, but said nothing as to the Senate being the judge of the elections, returns and qualifications of its members. Such resolution thus provided substantially for the procedure in Pennsylvania, whose upper house, or Council, ceased to be the judge of the elections and qualifications of its members when they ceased to be elective. On May 31st, Mr. Spaight moved an amendment to paragraph 5 so as to provide for the election of the Senators by the state legislatures. After some discussion, Mr. Spaight withdrew his motion. Mr. Sherman favored a Senate to consist of one member from each state, elected by the state legislatures. Mr. Pinkney moved to strike out "nomination by the state legislatures" in the Virginia Plan. This motion was lost and a vote on the whole clause was also lost.

The proposition was again taken up on June 7 in the Committee of the Whole. Mr. Read proposed that the members of the Senate be appointed by the President, "out of a proper number of persons to be nominated by the individual legislatures." This proposition was lost for want of a second. Mr. Dickinson then moved that the Senate be appointed by the state legislatures and the motion was adopted. The June 13th report of the Committee of the Whole on the Virginia Plan did not contain the provision that each House should be the judge of the elections, returns and qualifications of its members, nor did it refer to the question of expulsion. The New Jersey Plan, offered on June 15, as a substitute for the Virginia Plan, likewise contained no provision authorizing either of the Houses to be judge of the election, etc., of its members, or as to expulsion of members. Hamilton's first plan, submitted on June 18, did not contain either of these two provisions, but his plan, formulated later and near the end of the Convention, did contain a provision that each House should be the judge of the elections, returns and qualifications of its members, but expressly denied to the Senate the power to expel a member. The alleged Pinkney Plan provided that the lower house should be the judge of the elections, returns and qualifications of its own members, but was silent as to the Senate. No reason was given by Pinkney for the difference between the powers of the two Houses as to the elections, returns and qualifications of their members, but this was probably due to the fact that he had proposed that the Senators be elected by the lower House.

The report of the Committee on Detail on August 6 contained the provision in Article VI, Section 4, that "each house shall be the judge of the elections, returns and qualifications of its members," and, in Section 6, the provision that "each house may expel a member." Section 4 was agreed to in Convention on August 10, without discussion, showing that the membership of the Constitutional Convention considered such jurisdiction and power, except as limited in the Constitution, to be the same jurisdiction and power long exercised in England and in the separate colonies. The limitation is important, for the Constitution subsequently fixed the qualifications for membership in the House of Representatives and in the Senate, and the effect of this will be hereinafter discussed. Mr. Madison objected to the provision that each House may expel a member and observed that the right of expulsion "was too important to be exercised by a bare majority of a quorum; *and in emergencies of faction, might be dangerously abused.*"

To this wise warning the times now give proof.

He moved that "with the concurrence of two-thirds" be inserted between "may" and "expel." The motion was adopted and the resolution was referred to the Committee on Style, who reported it on September 12 as it now stands in Article I, Section 5, of the Constitution.

Let me, therefore, now recite the pertinent provisions of the Constitution. They require little, if any, gloss. They are written in words of common speech, whose meaning is so clear that "he who runs may read." These provisions, as indeed all provisions of the Constitution, are stated with an admirable and lucid simplicity that has made this document the admiration of the world.

CHAPTER IV

THE PROVISIONS OF THE CONSTITUTION

FOLLOWING its noble preamble, the Constitution begins:

ARTICLE I.

All legislative Powers herein granted shall be vested in a Congress of the United States, which shall consist of a Senate and House of Representatives.

The House of Representatives shall be composed of Members chosen every second year by the People of the several States, and the Electors in each State shall have the Qualifications requisite for Electors of the most numerous Branch of the State Legislature.

No Person shall be a Representative who shall not have attained to the Age of twenty-five Years, and been seven Years a Citizen of the United States, and who shall not, when elected, be an Inhabitant of that State in which he shall be chosen.

It will be noted that the members of the House of Representatives are to be selected "by the people of the several States," and the only limitation in this selection upon such right is the constitutional requirement that "the electors in each State shall have the qualifications requisite for electors of the most numerous branch of the State Legislature."

Then follows Section 3 of Article I:

The Senate of the United States shall be composed of two Senators from each State, chosen by the Legislature thereof, for six years; and each Senator shall have one vote.

Immediately after they shall be assembled in consequence of the first Election, they shall be divided as equally as may be into three classes. The seats of the Senators of the first class shall be vacated at the expiration of the second year, of the second class at the expiration of the fourth year, and of the third class at the expiration of the sixth year, so that one-third may be chosen every second year; and if vacancies happen by resignation, or otherwise, during the recess of the Legislature of any State, the Executive thereof may make temporary Appointments until the next meeting of the Legislature, which shall then fill such vacancies.

It will be noted that the Constitution thus expressly provides that the Senators of a State shall be "chosen by the Legislature thereof." This provision acquires additional significance when we recall that in the Constitutional Convention it was first proposed that the legislatures of the several States should only nominate a list of eligibles, and that the Federal House of Representatives or the President should make the final selection from such list. This was abandoned, and the sole requisite of a Senator, so far as his selection was concerned, was that he was to be "chosen by the Legislature thereof."

Any other theory would have been inconsistent with the political traditions of the American people. When the first Continental Congress met in 1774, no idea would have been more preposterous than that the Congress should have any veto power upon the members who constituted it, and who had been selected by each of the Colonies in its own way. The same is true of the second Continental Congress, which functioned under the Articles of Confederation. The Confederacy, which conducted the Revolutionary War and achieved our independence, would have quickly dissolved if the delegates of all the thirteen Colonies had presumed to dictate to any one Colony who its representatives in the Congress should be. Imagine the Continental Congress attempting to expel Dr. Franklin because of his heterodoxy, or Washington becaues he was a landowner.

Therefore, the words "chosen by the Legislature thereof," are but a reaffirmation of a great principle, without which the

United States would never have come into existence. Let it be remembered, that when the Constitution was formed, the Sovereign States were the creators and not the created.

Now follows the first interference by the Constitution with the right of a State to select any representative it saw fit, for the next paragraph of Section 3 reads as follows:

> No person shall be a Senator who shall not have attained to the age of thirty years, and been nine years a citizen of the United States, and who shall not, when elected, be an inhabitant of that State for which he shall be chosen.

Then follows this provision:

> The times, places and manner of holding elections for Senators and Representatives, shall be prescribed in each State by the Legislature thereof; but the Congress may at any time by law make or alter such regulations, except as to the place of choosing Senators.

Here again was an affirmation of the principle that the States should determine the manner of selecting their representatives, although, for the first time, the Congress is empowered to regulate, as to the members of the House, the "times, places and manner of holding elections," and as to the Senate, the "times and manner." This, however, only refers to the machinery of elections, and cannot be justly construed as in any way limiting a State's right to select its own Senators. This will be discussed hereafter.

Then follows the most important provision in this controversy:

> Each House shall be the judge of the elections returns and qualifications of its own members, and a majority of each shall constitute a quorum to do business; but a smaller number may adjourn from day to day, and may be authorized to compel the attendance of absent members, in such manner, and under such penalties as each House may provide.

This provision unquestionably invests each House with the right to determine whether a man, who claims to have been elected to either House, was in fact elected, and if so, whether he possesses the requisite qualifications, but these qualifications are obviously those which have already been prescribed in the Constitution as to age, the period of his citizenship, and the fact that he is an inhabitant of the State which he seeks to represent. To hold that "qualifications" has a broader meaning, and invests the right in either House to determine whether the chosen representative of the State is in other respects fit to take his seat, would be a nullification of the right of the people in each State to select their representatives, and the right of the Legislature of each State to select the Senators. It is preposterous to claim that the word "qualifications" means intellectual or moral fitness, for if this were so, the rights of the States to be represented in the Congress in their own way would be reduced to the vanishing point. In such event, the States would simply *nominate* a representative in the Senate, and the Senate would pass upon his fitness, and this, as already shown, was the very proposition that was voted down in the Constitutional Convention when it was proposed that, as to members of the Senate, the legislatures of the States should merely nominate an eligible list and the Federal House of Representatives should then make the final selection.

Then follows a very significant paragraph of Section 5:

> Each House may determine the rules of its proceedings, punish its members for disorderly behavior, and, with the concurrence of two thirds, expel a member.

It is very significant that the power of expulsion is dealt with in a different paragraph from the power given to the Senate and the House in the preceding paragraph, to determine whether one, who claims to have been elected, has in fact been elected, and if so, whether he possesses the "qualifications" which are prescribed in the Constitution. The two powers are distinct, and this is not merely indicated by the fact that they are dealt with in separate paragraphs, but by the even more significant fact that, while the question of an election and of the possession of the constitutional qualifications may be determined by a majority vote, the right to expel a member who has been given his seat requires a two-thirds vote.

The scope and extent of the right of expulsion has been little discussed and rarely defined, for the reason that few attempts have ever been made to exercise this power. Such a power runs so counter to all our precedents of Anglo-Saxon liberty, that it has been rarely invoked.

The clause in question must be read from its four corners, and in the light of the great controversy in England which gave it birth.

In my judgment, the power of expulsion refers to some act of a Senator *during his membership of the Senate,* and the act must have some reference to the discipline of the Senate.

This is indicated by the words "punish its members for disorderly behavior." If a member persistently violated the rules of the Senate, and that body could no longer effectively function because of his deliberate interference with its labors, then the Senate, if it is to continue to exist, must have the power to preserve its discipline, and to do so, must have the power to punish the member "for disorderly behavior." The final sentence in the paragraph indicates that expulsion was contemplated as possible punishment, but such punishment was so extreme that it was wisely provided that, while ordinary punishment could be imposed by a majority of the Senate, the final punishment of expulsion must have the concurrence of two-thirds.

It may be—but I do not concede it—that if a Senator during the period of his service, is proved to have been guilty of some crime, he can be expelled, even though the crime has no relation to the discipline of the Senate.

It is, however, equally clear, that the act which would justify his expulsion, must have taken place since his election. What he did prior to his election and qualification has been passed upon by the people of his State. In a political sense, it is *res adjudicata.* A candidate for the Senate might have been guilty of embezzlement before his election, but the right of the people of that State to send an embezzler to the Senate, if it sees fit, is clear. Such decision is the sole right of the State.

It must not be supposed that the general grant of power to each branch of Congress to determine the "qualifications" of its members gives them an unlimited discretion in determining the question of membership in the body. The general language which the Constitution uses must be read in connection with the entire instrument and, thus read, it is unreasonable that the power to judge of the "qualifications" of its own members was, or is, intended to destroy the rights of the States to select their own representatives in Congress.

The Supreme Court has said, in the case of U. S. v. Ballin, 144 U. S. 1:

> "The Constitution empowers each house to determine times and rules of proceedings. It may not by its rules ignore constitutional restraints, or violate fundamental rights, and there should be a reasonable relation between the mode or method of proceeding established by the rule and the result which is sought to be attained."

To permit the Senate to expel a Senator on the ground that, before his election, he had been either a fool or a knave, would revolutionize our theory of constitutional government. All this had been passed upon before the Constitution was framed in the great John Wilkes controversy.

The next pertinent provision is the last paragraph of Section 6, which reads as follows:

> No Senator or Representative shall, during the time for which he was elected be appointed to any civil office under the authority of the United States, which shall have been created, or the emoluments whereof shall have been encreased during such time; and no person holding any office under the United States, shall be a Member of either House during his continuance in office.

Here is another express limitation upon the power of the State to select a representative. It may not send a federal office holder to Congress.

These are all the pertinent provisions in the Constitution, as originally drafted, but in the amendments we will find two very significant changes.

The first is Article X:

ARTICLE X.

The powers not delegated to the United States by the Constitution, nor prohibited by it to the States, are reserved to the States respectively, or to the people.

As the Constitution had limited the power of the State to select its own representatives in Congress by four qualifications, hereinbefore referred to, it follows, under the Tenth Amendment, and would equally follow if there were no Tenth Amendment, that in all other respects the power of the States, which created the United States, to select their own representatives in their own way, was reserved to them. In other words, the Tenth Amendment was the explicit statement of the familiar maxim—*"Expressio unius est exclusio alterius."*

Then follows the Fourteenth Amendment, which was the result of the Civil War. Section 3 is especially pertinent. It reads as follows:

SECTION 3. No person shall be a Senator or Representative in Congress, or elector of President and Vice-President, or hold any office, civil or military, under the United States, or under any State, who, having previously taken an oath, as a member of Congress, or as an officer of the United States, or as a member of any State legislature, or as an executive or judicial officer of any State, to support the Constitution of the United States, shall have engaged in insurrection or rebellion against the same, or given aid or comfort to the enemies thereof. But Congress may by a vote of two-thirds of each House, remove such disability.

While this Section is no longer of any practical importance, as the disability which it imposed upon those who supported the war of secession has long since been removed, yet the

Section is of the greatest significance in this controversy in showing that *it required a constitutional amendment to invest the Senate with the right to exclude any one, even though he had engaged in a war to destroy the United States.*

The implication is inevitable that, in the absence of such a constitutional amendment, neither the Senate nor the House could exclude any representative of a seceding State on this ground. Thus if Mississippi, after the close of the Civil War, had sent Jefferson Davis to the Senate, the Senate would have had no power to expel him, if this section had not been incorporated in the Constitution. If it had been thought in that great constitutional crisis that the Senate had a general power to exclude any elected Senator on the ground of treason—and what ground could be greater?—then Section 3 would have been wholly unnecessary.*

Finally, we have the Seventeenth Amendment, which reads as follows:

ARTICLE XVII.

The Senate of the United States shall be composed of two Senators from each State, *elected by the people thereof,* for six years; and each Senator shall have one vote. The electors in each State shall have the qualifications requisite for electors of the most numerous branch of the State legislatures.

When vacancies happen in the representation of any State in the Senate, the executive authority of such State shall issue writs of election to fill such vacancies: *Provided,* That the legislature of any State may empower the executive thereof to make temporary appointments until the people fill the vacancies by election as the legislature may direct.

Here it will be noted that the Constitution expressly says that the Senators from each State shall be "elected by the

---

* During the Civil War, the Senate expelled two members (Bright of Indiana and Thomas of Maryland) who were charged with treasonable communications with the Confederacy, but this fairly related to the discipline of the Senate and in any event is explained by the conditions of a Civil War.

people thereof." It only interferes with the manner of the election in its provision that the electors in each State shall have the qualifications requisite for electors of the most numerous branch of the State Legislatures. Otherwise, the peoples of the State may have such election laws as they think proper, provided, of course, that they do not offend the Fifteenth Amendment as to race or color, and the Nineteenth Amendment as to sex. In other respects, the State is left free. It may have a primary law, or no primary law. It may have a property qualification, or no property qualification.

The author has thus quoted every pertinent provision of the Constitution. Reading them together, it seems too clear for argument, that each State has the right to select from its people any representative in the Senate that it sees fit, irrespective of his intellectual or moral qualifications, and that the only limitations upon such choice are, that he shall be thirty years of age, a citizen of the United States for at least nine years, an inhabitant of the State, and that he shall not hold any office under the United States, and that he shall not have engaged in insurrection or rebellion against the United States, or given aid or comfort to the enemies thereof, unless in the latter contingency, the Congress, by a vote of two-thirds, shall remove such disability.

In all other respects the right of the State is absolute and unimpaired. A State may have selected a member of the Senate or secured his nomination by unworthy means. He may have spent more to secure such nomination than many would think proper or legitimate. He may be intellectually unfitted for the high office, and his moral character may, in other respects, leave much to be desired.

The people of the United States may justifiably think that the State has sent to Congress an unfit man, who could add nothing to its deliberations, and whose influence may well be pernicious. None the less, the State has the right to send him. *It is its sole concern, and to nullify its choice is to destroy the basic right of a Sovereign State, and amounts to a revolution.*

In this matter we must not be pragmatists. If the Senate has the right to nullify the action of a Sovereign State in this matter for good reasons, it has equally the right to nullify it for bad reasons. The State may send a representative to the Senate, who has the intellectual ability of Webster, and the unimpeachable morality of George Washington, but he may be a member of a political party which, at the time, is in a minority. If the Senate rejects such a man it is possible that the plain usurpation of the power of the State cannot be questioned in any judicial proceeding. The sole remedy may be, as in the case of John Wilkes, in an appeal to the people, but while the victim might represent the majority of the people of his State, his party's representation in the Senate might well be only a minority, and thus, the right of one State to select its own representative could be nullified as long as a majority of the Senate, composed of the representatives of other States, saw fit to refuse him his credentials, or as long as two-thirds of the Senate saw fit to expel him.

*If such a power exists, then the greatest of all States' rights has become little more than a "scrap of paper." ***

* As to Art. I, Section 5, it appears that of the eleven States possessing written Constitutions in 1787, seven States, viz., Delaware, Maryland, Massachusetts, New Hampshire, New York, North Carolina, Pennsylvania, explicitly made either one or both Houses of the Legislature "judges of the qualifications and election" of their members; and New York and South Carolina gave to their State Legislatures also the powers previously actually exercised by the Colonial Legislatures. In no one of the State Constitutions is there any intimation that the word "qualifications" meant anything more than the qualifications expressly required in the respective Constitutions to attach to members of the Houses or House. In one of the above State Constitutions, the word "qualifications" is specifically limited by the addition of the words, "as pointed out in the Constitution." (See Massachusetts Constitution of 1780.)

CHAPTER V

THE PRIMA FACIE VALIDITY OF CERTIFICATES OF ELECTION

THE principle is well established that a newly-elected Senator is entitled to take the oath and to be admitted to his seat in the Senate when "he brings with him or presents a credential consisting of the certificate of his due election from the Executive of his state." The reason was thus stated by the late Senator Hoar, as Chairman of the Committee on Privileges and Elections, in the case of Senator Smoot:

> "If there were any other procedure, the result would be that a third of the Senate might be kept out of their seats for an indefinite length of time, on the presenting of objection without responsibility and never established before the Senate by any judicial inquiry. The result of this might be that a change in the political power of this government, which the people desired to accomplish, would be indefinitely postponed."

Senator Smoot was allowed to take his seat and the subsequent proceeding was a fruitless attempt to expel him. The vote vindicated his right to the seat.

The action in the case of Senator Smoot was in accordance with long-established precedent. One of the earlier cases was that of Senator Robbins in 1833, whose certificate of election was in proper form and there was no question as to his age, residence or inhabitancy of Rhode Island, the state from which he was chosen. His election was challenged and the debate on his right to take the oath of office is found in 10 Congressional Debates, Part I, pages 2-11.

A case in 1857 was that of Senator Graham N. Fitch, whose

election by the legislature of the State of Indiana had been challenged. Among other similar cases are those of George Goldthwaite, L. Q. C. Lamar, Henry A. DuPont, John T. Morgan, Lafayette Grover, John W. Smith, William Lorimer, Isaac Stephenson, Truman Newberry, Smith W. Brookhart and Earle B. Mayfield.

The rule is too well settled to be now seriously questioned that where a Senator-elect presents a certificate of election in proper form and possesses the qualifications of age, residence and inhabitancy named in the Constitution, he is *prima facie* entitled to his seat. Subsequent proceedings to vacate his seat must impeach the regularity of his election.

The Constitution requires, as hereinbefore stated, that a Senator be thirty years of age, nine years a resident of the United States, and an inhabitant of the State from which he is chosen; and he must not hold any other office under the United States. Other than the disqualifications stated in the Fourteenth Amendment, in reference to participation in the Civil War, these are all of the qualifications prescribed by the Constitution. The motions and resolutions in the Constitutional Convention to restrict seats in the Senate to native-born citizens of the United States and to require them to possess other qualifications, failed of adoption.

Mr. Justice Story stated in his classic work on the Constitution (5th Edition, pages 460-463) that neither the Congress of the United States, nor the States could superadd any qualifications to those prescribed in the Constitution for membership in the Senate and in the House of Representatives. He said:

> "It would seem but fair reasoning upon the plainest principles of interpretation that when the Constitution so established certain qualifications as necessary for office, it meant to exclude all others as prerequisites. From the very nature of such a provision, the affirmation of these qualifications would seem to imply a negation of all others."

The Senate adopted this view as early as 1855, in seating Lyman Trumbull of Illinois, whose seat had been challenged on the ground that he had been elected a judge of the State Court for a term which had not expired at the date of his election to the Senate. He had resigned two years prior to his election and the State Constitution had provided that no person could be elected to an office within two years after the expiration of his term of office. Senator Crittenden said, in his speech on March 3, 1856, in answer to the minority views that qualifications for Senators could be superadded to those specified in the Constitution:

"According to the plain meaning of the Federal Constitution, every inhabitant of a state, thirty years of age, who has been nine years a citizen of the United States, is eligible to the office of Senator. What more can be said about it? It is now supposed by those who contend that Mr. Trumbull is not entitled to his seat that it is competent for a state, by its Constitution—and I suppose they would equally contend by any law which the legislature might from time to time pass—to superadd additional qualifications. The Constitution of the United States, they say, has only in part regulated the subject, and therefore it is no interference with that Constitution to make additional regulations.

This, I think it will be plain to all, is a mere sophism when you come to consider it. If it was a power within the regulation of, and proper to be regulated by, the Constitution of the United States, and if that Constitution has qualified it, as I have stated, prescribing the age, prescribing the residence, prescribing the citizenship, was there anything more intended? If so, the framers of the Constitution would have said so. The very enumeration of these qualifications excludes the idea that they intended any other qualifications."

It was so well settled by the Trumbull case that qualifications could not be superadded to those enumerated in the Constitution for Senators that the late Senator Knox, with entire accuracy, stated in the course of his speech of February 14, 1907, on the floor of the Senate in support of Senator Smoot's right to his seat, that:

"He (Senator Smoot) was at the time of his election over thirty years of age and had been nine years a citizen of the United States, and when elected was an inhabitant of Utah. These are the only qualifications named in the Constitution and it is not in our power to say to the State, 'These are not enough; we require other qualifications', or to say that we cannot trust the judgment of the states in the selection of Senators, and we therefore insist upon the right to disapprove them for any reason."

The late Senator Knox deservedly enjoyed a great reputation as a constitutional lawyer and he was speaking from a record of precedents, which had slowly accumulated since the famous case of John Wilkes, when he declared that no qualifications for Senators could be superadded to those specified in the Constitution.

The right of a State to equal representation and vote in the councils of the Nation was one of the great compromises of the Constitutional Convention. A passing knowledge of the struggles of the Convention at Philadelphia and in the ratifying State conventions is sufficient to demonstrate that the Constitution could never have been either framed or ratified, had there been any idea in the minds of the leaders of that period that a State might be deprived of its equal representation and vote in the Senate and what is of equal, if not greater, importance, the right itself to select its representative. It was stated by the Supreme Court of the United States in the Newberry case (256 U. S. 243), where an attempt was made to convict Senator Newberry under an invalid Federal Statute designed to regulate primary election of Senators, that:

"The history of the times indicates beyond reasonable doubt that if the Constitution makers had claimed for this section the latitude we are now asked to sanction, it would not have been ratified."

Subject to the qualifications as to age, citizenship and inhabitancy, the State assumes a responsibility for the fitness and character of the Senators elected to represent them. As

Senator Knox eloquently stated, in the above referred to address:

> "The perfection of human liberties under law will only be attained under the American Constitution when each of the dual sovereignties within its sphere exerts its powers to the utmost limits for the public weal; when the States and the artificial bodies they have created cease to deny and resist the rightful and full exercise of the National power over National affairs; when there is no attempt to encroach upon the undeniable reserved powers of the States for the aggrandizement of National power; when the people discriminate between wise policies designed to meet the imperative needs of modern conditions, and demagogic assaults upon the foundations of the Republic for political and personal purposes; when the people shall not be vexed by unnecessary legislation about their daily affairs, and normal conditions are undisturbed by ceaseless agitations, agitations fomented by ignorance and insincerity and misrepresenting those just and constitutional policies of the time, which had a due beginning, have a reason for their existence and shall have a due ending, when their work is accomplished."

The historical background of the Constitution leaves no room for reasonable doubt that the Constitution does not authorize the Senate to go back of the election and return of a Senator in order to pass upon his previous conduct, either moral or otherwise. The electors are the sole and exclusive judges of a Senator's conduct prior to his election. If they see fit to elect him, notwithstanding alleged delinquencies, there is no power under the Constitution to expel him, and it certainly cannot be argued that in this or any respect the Senate is the censor of the morals of the American people.

This principle was established in the early days of the Republic in the case of Humphrey Marshall. The Senate was then composed of many members who had sat either in the Constitutional Convention at Philadelphia, or in the State ratifying conventions, or in both. Marshall had been charged with a crime under the laws of Kentucky, alleged to have been committed prior to his election. The charge was referred to a Senate Committee and it reported that the Senate had no jurisdiction, saying:

> "If, in the present case, the party has been guilty in the manner suggested, no reason has been alleged by the memoralist why he has not long since been tried in the state and district where he committed the offense. Until he is legally convicted, the principles of the Constitution and of the common law concur in presuming that he is innocent."

The principle was so well established in 1893 that the Senate refused to take any action in the case of William N. Roach, who had been elected a Senator from North Dakota and whose seat had been challenged on the ground that, prior to his election, he had embezzled a sum of money from the Citizens National Bank, of Washington, D. C. Senator Roach admitted that he had been short in his accounts, but alleged that he had repaid a part of the shortage.

Assault was made on the principle during the bitter political struggles between Jefferson and Hamilton, and later during the period when passions ran high over the conduct of Aaron Burr. John Smith, a Senator from the State of Ohio, had been indicted as an accomplice in the alleged treasonable designs of Aaron Burr. The indictment had been dismissed following the trial of Burr, but the Senate appointed a committee to inquire into the charges against him, and this committee unanimously reported a resolution of expulsion. However, the Senate refused to adopt the resolution. The Senate Committee criticized the action taken in the case of Marshall, but this criticism was unnecessary, for the reason that the charge against Marshall concerned his alleged conduct before his election to the Senate, while the charge against Smith concerned his conduct after his election to the Senate.

The Senate may have power to judge a Senator for acts committed after his election and when, for six years, he is beyond the control of the electors (as in the case of William Blount, in 1784, who was expelled for a high misdemeanor), without conceding that the Senate has the power to judge of acts committed by a Senator prior to election and which his constituents presumably disregarded in electing him to the Senate.

A third case in which the principle was sustained that the Senate was not concerned with the alleged acts of Senators prior to their election was that of Isaac Stephenson. It was found as a fact that at least $107,000 had been spent in support of his candidacy for nomination for Senator in the Wisconsin primary. This was in 1909 and prior to the Seventeenth Amendment to the Constitution, which authorized the election of Senators by popular vote. There was also failure to keep detailed accounts of expenditures, the destruction of memoranda relating to the primary, the shifting of records and papers concerning the primary from one place to another to avoid the Senate Committee. The reports of the Committee were not placed on the ground that the Senate had neither jurisdiction nor power to expel Stephenson for something that occurred prior to his election by the State Legislature, but it is equally true that the historical background of the provision of the Constitution, authorizing the Senate to judge the elections, returns and qualifications of its members, the history of the provision in the Constitutional Convention, and the precedents in the Senate united in establishing that principle.

The Senate is not above the law and is neither authorized nor justified in ignoring its decisions in prior similar cases, much less the plain meaning of the Constitution and the history of any provision, under which it purports to act in judging an election in some subsequent case.

It was charged in the case of Henry B. Payne, who was elected a Senator from Ohio in 1885, that certain members of the State Legislature had been bribed to vote for him. The Senate Investigating Committee referred to the first and second clauses of Article I, Section 5, of the Constitution, and said:

> "As these two ends alone limit the basis and object of any investigation proposed, either for invalidating the election of a Senator or expelling from the Senate a duly

elected and qualified member of it, a scrutiny of the grounds, in fact, upon which such action is demanded, in any case arising, from the Senate requires an ascertainment whether the scope of the proposition and the testimony presented, or reasonably assumed, would justify the ultimate action of the Senate under one or the other of these clauses of the Constitution. . . .

The integrity of the election, and not of the member, is in question under this clause of the Constitution.

But, on the same reason, the investigation, which now deals with the election as vitiated, and not the member as innocent, must reach the proof that the fraud, corruption, or bribery embraces enough in number of the voting electors to have changed, by these methods, the result of the election. If these corrupted votes gave the innocent member his seat, the deprivation of these corrupted votes vacates his seat, however innocent he is. But if the uncorrupted votes were adequate to his election, and he is purged from complicity in the fraud, corruption, or bribery, his seat is not exposed to any question of validity in the election."

A similar charge of bribery was made in the case of John J. Ingalls, who was elected a Senator from Kansas in 1876. The Senate Investigating Committee reported as follows:

"*Resolved*, That the testimony taken by the Committee proves that bribery and other corrupt means were employed by persons favoring the election of Hon. John J. Ingalls to the Senate to obtain for him the votes of members of the Legislature of Kansas in the Senatorial election in that state. But it is not proved by the testimony that enough votes were secured by such means to determine the result of the election in his favor. Nor is it shown that Senator Ingalls authorized acts of bribery to secure his election."

The principle had been so well established that in the case of Senator Lorimer the following colloquy took place on the floor of the Senate:

"Mr. Bailey. It is not probable, sir, that the people of this country could be persuaded under any circumstances to adopt or approve a law which would vitiate a senatorial election on account of the ineffective misconduct of some irresponsible person, and certainly they would not be so foolish as to do so with an amendment now pending before us to provide for the election of Senators by direct vote of the people. If that amendment shall finally be adopted—and it will sooner or later—the Senate of the United States, under the rule proposed by the Senator from Indiana, would be perpetually engaged in the trial of contested-election cases, for in every state of this Union some wretch can be found so base as to sell his vote and then confess his crime, if by doing so he could invalidate an election which has gone against the interest or the wishes of his confederates. Indeed, sir, desperate and unscrupulous politicians would deliberately plan to buy a few votes for the opposition so that if the election did not result in their favor they could prove the corruption, and thus defeat their opponents in that way, when they could not do so at the polls. The successful candidate might receive a majority of the honest votes running into the thousands, or the tens of thousands, and yet under this rule a few scoundrels could set aside the clearest and most unequivocal expression of the popular will. A rule which invites that, or a rule which permits that, is too absurd to require a serious consideration at this time and in this place.

Mr. President, perhaps I can save time and relieve the Senate from a tedious examination of the authorities by coming to an agreement with the Senators who have participated in this debate as to the law which must govern us in deciding this case. It is not necessary for me to interrogate the Senator from Tennessee (Mr. Frazier), because in the brief, but very clear, statement of his views he has laid down the law exactly as I understand it, and there is absolutely no difference between him and me in that respect. Nor can I believe that there is any difference on this proposition between me and the Senators from New York, Idaho, and Iowa; and for the purpose of dispensing with an argument in support of my view, I believe that I will venture upon the unusual course of asking those Senators in the open Senate whether or not we can agree upon the law. I will first ask the Senator from New York whether he assents to my legal proposition, that—

If the officer whose election is challenged did not personally participate in, or encourage, or sanction the bribery, then his election can not be avoided unless it is shown by sufficient evidence that enough votes were bribed to affect the result.

Does the Senator from New York assent to that proposition?

Mr. Root. I do not.

Mr. Bailey. Then I will produce abundant authorities to show that it is the law. I will next ask the Senator from Idaho whether he agrees that I have stated the law correctly.

Mr. Borah. Mr. President—

The Presiding Officer. Does the Senator from Texas yield to the Senator from Idaho?

Mr. Bailey. I do.

Mr. Borah. If I correctly understand the statement of the Senator—it is pretty difficult to follow a statement as it is made and analyze it at the same time—I do agree to that legal proposition so far as this case is concerned. But permit me, in order that I may not be found in error in the Record to-morrow again, to ask the Senator a question, and that is whether or not the statement that I now make is the same statement that he makes: If the officer whose election is challenged did not personally participate in or encourage or sanction the bribery, then his election can not be avoided unless it is shown by sufficient evidence that enough votes were bribed, without which bribed votes he would not have had the majority required by the statute.

Mr. Bailey. It is in effect the same: and if there is any difference, the Senator has stated the law a little stronger on my side than I have stated it. The only difference between the Senator and myself will be as to the application of the rule. I perfectly understand that when we reach that point we will be at the parting of our ways, but on the law, I think there can be no difference.

Mr. Borah. If the statement I have just made is the

statement the Senator thinks is contained in his statement, it is the statement which I believe contains the law.

Mr. Bailey. There is no question about that, and I will now ask the Senator from Iowa if he agrees with me on the law as I have stated it.

Mr. Cummins. I stated with all the clearness that I could when I was discussing this matter some days ago my view of the law. I believe it to be true that if the evidence fails to show on the part of the Senator any personal participation in or knowledge of corrupt practices with which the election may be charged, then in order to invalidate the election it must be shown that the election was accomplished by and through bribery or corruption.

Mr. Bailey. I am gratified to know that there is no difference between me and the Senators from Iowa and Idaho on the law; and I am confident that upon a further reflection the Senator from New York will withdraw his dissent, for the rule has been long and uniformly followed here.

Mr. Root. I do not want the Senator from Texas to consider that I dissent from all and every part of his statement. As I listened to it, it appeared to me that it was capable of a construction which would make it broader than I think ought to be. I will gladly examine the statement, as it will appear in the Record, I suppose, and see whether I wish to suggest a qualification."

It necessarily follows that, if bribery in the *election* of a Senator does not disqualify him, unless sufficient votes have been purchased to influence the election, and unless the Senator-elect had personal knowledge and was a participant in such bribery, it cannot be held that large expenditures in a primary, which is no part of the "election," disqualifies him.

The system of nominations for candidacy at elections was known and practiced in many of the thirteen Colonies, both before and after the Declaration of Independence. A system of nomination by political parties of candidates for election of Senators by state legislatures was known and practiced when the Seventeenth Amendment was adopted, transferring such elections from the state legislatures to the electorate of the states. Both the Constitution, as it was originally drafted in 1787, and the subsequent Seventeenth Amendment are equally silent in the matter of nominations of United States Senators.

The majority of the Senate Committee reported in the case of Senator Stephenson that:

> "When we speak of the election of a United States Senator under existing constitutional and legislative provisions, we contemplate only the election by the legislature of the state. There is, as yet, no recognition to be given extra-legislative proceedings in the matter of what is termed 'direct primaries', no such method of selection being recognized by the law of the United States. . . .
>
> The direct primary, legally speaking, is no part of an election of a United States Senator. The duty of an election of a Senator does not, under any law, rest with the electorate, but is vested by the Constitution solely in the legislature. The legislature electing had no existence until after the general election. The nomination of such members at the primary vested in the nominees not even an inchoate right. . . .
>
> The question arises, can any act in controvention of a law that is absolutely void work a forfeiture of any right to an office vested through the compliance with the Constitution and the laws of the United States? Did the proceedings preceding and at the direct primary relative to a choice for a United States Senator amount to more than a 'straw vote'?"

A Senate Committee also reported in 1885, in the case of Henry B. Payne, that:

> "The State should execute its laws respecting the purity of Senatorial elections by the indictment and conviction of a single person who bribes or is bribed, whether the election is affected or not. The State should investigate as well to the end of better laws and surer execution of the laws. The State, too, is charged with the maintenance of 'the honor of Ohio', and its vindication rests with its own legislature, its own judiciary, and its

own people; but it cannot demand this vindication at the
hands of the United States Senate, except as that may
flow from investigations by that body within the limits
of its constitutional power and duties."

That the majority of the Committee in the case of Senator
Stephenson was composed of able constitutional lawyers, and
that the action of the Senate in refusing to expel Senator
Stephenson for alleged irregularities in the primaries was in
accordance with the Constitution, is attested by the subsequent
decision of the Supreme Court of the United States in the
Newberry case. This most important decision, which held
that the federal Government had no delegated power to legislate as to primary elections—at least prior to the Seventeenth
Amendment,—will be discussed more fully in a later chapter.
Moreover, it is a well-known fact that practically all State
primary election laws exclude from participation in any primary
of any political party such of the electorate as have not previously registered as members of that party. It is obvious
that a nomination by any political party of a candidate is, in
no sense of the term, an election, and confers on the nominee
not even an inchoate status as United States Senator. This is
true, even though nomination in some of the States, particularly
in the South, is equivalent to an election.

The change effected by the Seventeenth Amendment from
election by state legislatures to election by the voters of the
States, has not changed the principle stated in the Stephenson
case. Nor has it in any manner shifted the exclusive duty of
the State as set forth in the Senate report in the Payne case.

The reason for the lack of federal control over State primaries is clear. The framers of the Constitution deliberately
left the control of party nominations and political campaigns
to the people, where it has remained since the foundation of the
Government and where such control had been long before either
the Declaration of Independence or the Constitutional Convention. The framers of the Constitution knew that any attempt to take from the people their control over nominations
of candidates, to be later elected to offices, would result in the

rejection of the Constitution. Even the power conferred by Article I, Section 4, to control the time, place and manner of the elections nearly resulted in the rejection of the Constitution.

The people of the States are fully competent to regulate primaries or conventions for the nomination of candidates for election to office, including nominations for Senator. They are also competent to punish in their courts any violations of such regulations. There have been too many attempts to regulate from Washington the morals of the people. As a result, many otherwise law-abiding people have such contempt for the regulations that there is danger of the structure of law and order falling in cureless ruin.

Any question centering around control of the Senate by one or the other political party, through the expulsion of members of the other party, tends inevitably to become a controversy in which the merits are secondary to considerations of party politics. This is no new fact. Anson, in his "Law and Custom of the English Constitution" (Vol. 1, page 170), thus illustrates the truth:

> "The closing struggles of Walpole's ministry, in December 1741, turned, not on his foreign or domestic policy, but on votes in the House of Commons taken on election petitions. 'Last Friday,' says Horace Walpole, 'we carried a Cornish election. You cannot imagine the zeal of the young men on both sides. Tuesday we met on the merits of the Westminster election, and at ten at night divided and lost it. They had 220 and we 216; so the election was declared void. We had 41 more members in town who would not, or could not, come down. *The time is a touchstone for wavering consciences.* All the arts, money, promises and threats, all the arts of a former year are applied and self interest operates to the aid of their party and the defeat of ours.' The merits of the disputed election troubled no one; the trial to conscience was the question of deserting a Minister, whose fall was clearly imminent. Finally, the loss of the Chippenham election petition determined Walpole to resign."

The House of Commons sought in 1770 to escape the evils of political judgments in contested elections by transferring the decision thereof to a committee and later to the courts. The framers of the American Constitution sought such escape by providing in the Constitution for a restricted decision as to the qualifications of members of the House and Senate which were carefully defined and by requiring a two-thirds vote for expulsion.

A Senate Committee recognized this as early as 1807, in reporting a resolution for the expulsion of Senator John Smith, which failed of adoption, that:

"The provision in our Constitution, which forbids the expulsion of a member by an ordinary majority and requires for this act of rigorous and painful duty, the assent of two-thirds, your Committee considers as a wise and sufficient guard against the possible abuse of this legislative discretion. In times of heat and violent party spirit, the rights of the minority might not always be duly respected, if a majority could expel their members under no other control than that of their discretion. The operation of this rule is of great efficiency, both over the proceedings of the whole body and over the conduct of every individual member. The times when the most violent struggles of contending parties occur—when the conflict of opposite passions is most prone to excess—are precisely the times when the members are most equally divided; when the majority amounts to the proportion of two-thirds, the security of its own strength is, of itself, a guard against extraordinary stretches of power; when the minority dwindles to the proportion of one-third, its consciousness of weakness dissuades from any attempt to encroach upon the rights of the majority, which might provoke retaliation."

When the prize is the control of the Senate and it can be gained· by the expulsion of one or more members, then the danger of the ruin of our institutions by the spirit of faction becomes great.

The danger was never better stated than in the following

quotation from the majority report of 1833, on the right of Senator Robbins to retain his seat in the Senate:

"Causes might arise to render the election voidable, and these are enumerated in the Constitution of the United States. We might inquire, Was the person elected thirty years of age at the time of his election? Had he been nine years a citizen of the United States? Was he, at the time of his election, a citizen of the state from which he shall have been chosen? Was the election held at the time and place directed by the laws of the state? These are facts capable of clear demonstration by proof, and in the absence of the requisite qualifications in either of the specified cases, or if the existing laws of the state regulating the time and place of holding the election were violated, the Senate, acting under the power to judge of the 'elections, returns and qualifications of its own members', might adjudge the commission of the person elected void; although in other respects it was legal and constitutional.

But where the sovereign will of the State is made known through its legislature and consummated by its proper official functionaries in due form, it would be a dangerous exertion of power to look behind the commission for defects in the component parts of the legislature, or in the peculiar organization of the body for reasons to justify the Senate in declaring its acts absolutely void. Such a power, if carried to its legitimate extent, would subject the entire scope of state legislation to be overruled by our decision, and even the right of suffrage of individual members of the legislature, whose elections were contested, might be set aside.

It would also lead into investigations into the motives of members in casting their votes, for the purpose of establishing a charge of bribery or corruption in particular cases. These matters, your Committee think, properly belong to the tribunals of the state and cannot constitute the basis on which the Senate could, without an infringement of state sovereignty, claim the right to declare the election of the Senator void, who possesses the requisite qualifications and was chosen according to the forms of law and the Constitution."

CHAPTER VI

THE FEDERAL REGULATION OF PRIMARY ELECTIONS

MANY thoughtful students of this constitutional question will agree with the definition of federal power over the elections for members of Congress, as set forth in the previous chapters. They may, however, differ as to the application of this definition to the coming controversy in the Senate. It will be suggested that the federal power to regulate the times and manner of elections for members of the Senate is sufficiently broad to include the regulation of primary elections. It will be contended that such "elections" are now a recognized part of the machinery of elections and have a legal status as such.

This is undoubtedly the crux of the problem.

The argument that will be made by those who may seek to nullify the elections of Mr. Vare and Mr. Smith may be stated in the following syllogism:

The major premise is that the Federal Government has the power to regulate the times and manner of elections for Senators.

The minor premise, which is in the nature of a *sequitur,* is that the Federal Government has power to regulate the conduct of primary contests, as an integral part of the legal machinery of elections.

The conclusion sought to be deduced will be that the Senate has the power either to refuse to accept the credentials in question, or, having accepted them, to expel.

This syllogism is open to two fatal objections.

The first is that the minor premise is untrue.

The second is that, if both premises were true, it does not follow that the Senate has the power in question. It is a clear *non-sequitur.*

Assuming that both premises were correct, the only conclusion would be that *Congress* would have power to pass a law which would regulate primary contests and which might, if Congress saw fit, limit the amount of money which a candidate or his friends could spend in his behalf.

Congress, as the law-making body, has not done so. The only law which it attempted to pass has been adjudged null and void by the Supreme Court of the United States in the Newberry case, to which reference will be made hereafter.

If the Congress has not seen fit, under any power which it may have under the Seventeenth Amendment, to make a regulation in respect to primary contests, then the Senate has no power to expel a Senator-elect on the ground that he or his friends spent an excessive amount of money in the primary contests. If such a rule were established, either by specific actions by the Senate in the Pennsylvania or Illinois cases, or by a general and permanent rule of the Senate, as proposed by Senator La Follette, the Senate would, in fact, legislate without the concurrence of the House of Representatives or the approval of the President, and it would superadd to the "qualifications" of Senators, as prescribed in the Constitution, a new qualification.

The distinction between the power of the legislative body to prescribe a *law* and the power of one branch of the Legislature to establish a *rule* to which members elected must conform, as a prerequisite to their election, was clearly set forth by Grenville in his famous speech in the Wilkes case.*

In that case, as previously shown, the House of Commons attempted to declare that Wilkes, because he had libeled a Minister of the Crown and violated a criminal law in publishing unlawful literature, was, *per se,* divested of his right to remain a member of the House of Commons. Grenville clearly pointed out that, while the *Parliament* could, by a duly enacted law, to which the theoretical assent of the Crown would be given, make such a regulation of the right to sit in the House of Commons, the House of Commons, itself, could not do so under the Constitution of England.

This reasoning is even more applicable to our Government,

* Hereafter quoted, pp. 88-89.

with its written Constitution and its carefully restricted delegation of power to the Federal Government. Assuming that power has been delegated by the Constitution to the Federal Government to regulate primary contests, such regulation must be passed by both the House of Representatives and the Senate and be approved by the President. If disapproved by the President, the proposed law has no efficacy, unless two-thirds of the House and the Senate pass the law over the President's veto. To permit the Senate, by a standing rule or specific resolution in the Pennsylvania and Illinois cases, to regulate primary contests by unseating any Senator-elect, who has failed to conform to the regulation, would be a clear usurpation of a power which the Senate can only enjoy in conjunction with the House of Representatives and the President.

Even though the conclusion in the proposed syllogism, as to the power of the Senate, were justified if both premises were sound, it remains to be shown that the minor premise is utterly unsound. It is no longer open to question that the federal power to regulate the "times and manner of elections for Senators" does not include any power to regulate primary contests. To argue this is unnecessary, in view of the decision of the Supreme Court of the United States—the final arbiter in matters of constitutional law—in the Newberry case, where it was held by a majority of the Court that such a law, which had been enacted prior to the Seventeenth Amendment, was null and void for want of constitutional power. It is true that Justice McKenna, who concurred in this decision, reserved the question as to whether such a law might now be enacted, in view of the provisions of the Seventeenth Amendment.

It is a significant fact that, although the Newberry decision was rendered on May 2, 1921, and a doubt was expressed by one Justice (McKenna) as to the possible existence of a legislative power to regulate primary contests under the Seventeenth Amendment, Congress has not passed any such law and, in the absence of any such law, it must be assumed that Congress preferred to observe the historic policy of the nation, which is to leave such questions to the exclusive regulation of the States.

This was undoubtedly the historic policy of America at the time of the adoption of the Constitution. The wise framers of that great charter of government recognized that even as to elections conditions would naturally differ and that election laws would require adaptation to their local necessities.

Suffrage was not regarded as a natural right. It was to be given or withheld as the common welfare prescribed. There was, indeed, the widest variance in respect to the right to vote among the thirteen Colonies. In many Colonies, the right was strictly limited to freeholders. In a few, the more liberal rule prevailed and men, who were not freeholders, but who had a legitimate stake in the community, were permitted to vote. Such diversity in conditions still exists.

The only interference by the Constitution with state control over elections was in the provisions above cited, that Congress could, if it saw proper, overrule the action of the state as to the "times, places and manner of holding elections." To prevent any discrimination between the right to vote when exercised for the election of state officers, and the right to vote when exercised for the election of federal officers, it was provided that the qualifications of electors in each state, in the matter of federal officers, should be the same as the qualifications of electors in such state, when they were electing the members of the more numerous branch of the State Legislature.

Further than that, the Constitution did not seek to go. It felt that each State could wisely determine whether the right to vote should be liberally extended or narrowly restricted. While the framers of the Constitution probably never conceived as a possibility the extension of the right to negroes, yet, if that possibility ever occurred to them, they presumably believed that each state could determine to better advantage what its own local conditions would justify in promoting the great objective of "the common welfare."

If the possibilities of the Fifteenth Amendment had ever suggested themselves to these sagacious statesmen, they would have said that, while a State with a relatively small negro population might without prejudice to the common welfare extend to them the privilege of voting, yet another State, where the negro population was ignorant and in a largely preponderating majority, might wisely deny such right.

Our Government has twice departed from this historic policy.

I shall not discuss, and do not express any opinion, as to whether either departure was a wise one. It is enough that the American people have so ordained.

Each departure was, however, the result of a cataclysmic convulsion. The Fifteenth Amendment, following the Civil War, prevented the states from discriminating against any citizen by reason of his color, and the Nineteenth Amendment, following the World War, made a similar provision with respect to sex.

Excepting these two departures from the original plan, it still remains as a fundamental feature of our political institutions that the Federal Government shall leave to the States in all other respects the right to control elections, saving only the supervisory power of Congress to modify such local regulations by a national law in respect to the "times, places and manner of holding elections for Senators and Representatives." It is important to note that neither this clause, nor the prohibition of discrimination in regard to color or sex in elections, attempted to interfere with *nominations* of candidates for election.

Even this restricted and purely supervisory power over elections was regarded with distrust by the generation that framed the Constitution. Their jealous love of home rule, and their distrust of the power of a central government to control them in the time, places and manner of elections, led many of them to object to the new Constitution on the ground that too much power was given to the central government. Thereupon, the proponents of the Constitution, in the great struggle for ratification, explained that the Constitution did not contemplate any vexatious interference with the reserved rights of the states in the matter of their elections, much less an attempt to dictate their choice of representatives in the Congress. Thus, in the debates in the Virginia Ratifying Convention, Madison—well called "The Father of the Constitution"—replied to Monroe:

> "It was found impossible to fix the time, place and manner of election of Representatives in the Constitution. It was found necessary to leave the regulation of these, in the first place, to the state governments as being best acquainted with the situation of the people, subject to the control of the general government, in order to enable it to produce uniformity and prevent its own dissolution. . . . Were they exclusively under the control of the state governments, the general government might easily be dissolved. But if they be regulated properly by the state legislatures the congressional control will probably never be exercised. The power appears to me satisfactory, and as unlikely to be abused as any part of the Constitution."

Hamilton, when he ably defended the new Constitution, gave, in the *Federalist* papers, the same explanation:

> "They (the convention) have submitted the regulation of elections for the Federal Government, in the first instance, to the local administrations; which, in ordinary cases, and when no improper views prevail, may be both more convenient and more satisfactory; but they have reserved to the national authority a right to interpose, whenever extraordinary circumstances might render that interposition necessary to its safety."

Commenting upon these provisions, Mr. Justice Clarke, speaking for the Supreme Court in the case of United States against Gradwell (243 U. S. p. 864), said:

> "With it thus clearly established that the policy of Congress for so great a part of our constitutional life has been, and now is, to leave the conduct of the election of its members to state laws, administered by state officers, and that whenever it has assumed to regulate such elections it has done so by positive and clear statutes, such as were enacted in 1870, it would be a strained and unreasonable

construction to apply to such elections this Section 37, originally a law for the protection of the revenue, and for now fifty years confined in its application to "Offenses against the Operations of the Government," as distinguished from the processes by which men are selected to conduct such operations."

Whatever may be said as to this question of constitutional power over elections, there can be no question as to the continuing policy of our Government since the formation of the Constitution.   With the exception of a few periods when party passion ran high, and with the exception of the two great crises in our national life, which gave rise to the Fifteenth and the Nineteenth Amendments, the national Government, almost continuously throughout our history, has adopted the wise policy of leaving these matters to the States.*

* This was strikingly shown by Mr. Justice Clarke, in his opinion in the Gradwell case, where he thus reviewed the legislative history of such federal regulation of state elections:

"Although Congress has had this power of regulating the conduct of congressional elections from the organization of the government, our legislative history upon the subject shows that except for about twenty-four of the one hundred and twenty-eight years since the government was organized, it has been its policy to leave such regulations almost entirely to the states, whose representatives Congressmen are.   For more than fifty years no congressional action whatever was taken on the subject, until 1842, when a law was enacted requiring that Representatives be elected by districts (5 Stat. at L. p. 491, chap. 47), thus doing away with the practice which had prevailed in some states of electing on a single state ticket all of the members of Congress to which the state was entitled.

"Then followed twenty-four years more before further action was taken on the subject, when Congress provided for the time and mode of electing United States Senators (14 Stat. at L. 243, chap. 245), and it was not until four years later, in 1870, that for the first time, a comprehensive system for dealing with congressional elections was enacted.   This system was comprised in Secs. 19-22 of the act approved May 31st, 1870 (16 Stat. at L. p. 144, chap. 114), in Secs. 5 and 6 of the act approved July 14, 1870 (16 Stat. at L. p. 254, chap. 254), and in the act amending and supplementing these acts, approved June 10, 1872 (17 Stat. at L. pp. 347-349, chap. 415).

"These laws provided extensive regulations for the conduct of congressional elections.   They made unlawful false registration, bribery, voting without legal right, making false returns of votes cast, interfering in any manner with officers of election, and the neglect by any such officer of any duty required of him by state or Federal law; they provided for appointment by circuit judges of the United States of persons to attend at places of registration and at elections, with

No significant departure from this policy was ever made until 1911, when Congress adopted the so-called Federal Corrupt Practices Act, which was declared null and void in the Newberry case and which reads as follows:

> "No candidate for Representative in Congress or for Senator of the United States shall give, contribute, expend, use, or promise, or cause to be given, contributed, expended, used, or promised, in procuring his nomination and election, any sum, in the aggregate, in excess of the amount which he may lawfully give, contribute, expend, or promise under the laws of the state in which he resides: Provided, That no candidate for Representative in Congress shall give, contribute, expend, use or promise any sum, in the aggregate, exceeding five thousand dollars in any campaign for his nomination and election; and no candidate for Senator of the United States shall give, contribute, expend, use, or promise any sum, in the aggregate, exceeding ten thousand dollars in any campaign for his nomination and election:
>
> "Provided further, That money expended by any such candidate to meet and discharge any assessment, fee, or

authority to challenge any person proposing to register or vote unlawfully, to witness the counting of votes, and to identify by their signatures the registration of voters and election tally sheets; and they made it lawful for the marshals of the United States to appoint special deputies to preserve order at such elections, with authority to arrest for any breach of the peace committed in their view.

"These laws were carried into the revision of the United States Statutes of 1873-74, under the title, "Crimes against the Elective Franchise and Civil Rights of Citizens," Rev. Stat. Secs. 5506 to 5532, inclusive.

"It will be seen from this statement of the important features of these enactments that Congress by them committed to Federal officers a very full participation in the process of the election of Congressmen, from the registration of voters to the final certifying of the results, and that the control thus established over such elections was comprehensive and complete. It is a matter of general as of legal history that Congress, after twenty-four years of experience, returned to its former attitude toward such elections, and repealed all of these laws with the exception of a few sections not relevant here. (Act approved February 8, 1894, 28 Stat. at L. p. 36, chap. 25, Comp. Stat. 1913, Sec. 1015.) This repealing act left in effect, as apparently relating to the elective franchise, only the provisions contained in the eight sections of chapter 3 of the Criminal Code, Secs. 19 to 26, inclusive, which have not been added to or substantially modified during the twenty-three years which have since elapsed."

charge made or levied upon candidates by the laws of the state in which he resides, or for his necessary personal expenses, incurred for himself alone, for travel and subsistence, stationery and postage, writing or printing (other than newspapers), and distributing letters, circulars, and posters, and for telegraph and telephone service, shall not be regarded as an expenditure within the meaning of this section, and shall not be considered any part of the sum herein fixed as the limit of expenses and need not be shown in the statements herein required to be filed."

It was under this statute that Truman H. Newberry, who had been elected by the State of Michigan to the Senate, was indicted and convicted, because of alleged illegal acts in the primary election. The Supreme Court set aside the conviction because of the invalidity of the statute.

The majority of the Court held that there was a clear distinction between the "election," which is a fixed and formal governmental process, and the activities of citizens in respect to such elections, such as the primary elections to select candidates and the general conduct of a campaign. As to these, the Supreme Court has decided that no power was given to the Federal Government, and this conclusion seems to the author of this book to be clearly demonstrated by the very able opinion of Mr. Justice McReynolds in the Newberry case.

Let me quote a few passages from this convincing opinion:

"If it be practically true that, under present conditions, a designated party candidate is necessary for an election,—a preliminary thereto,—nevertheless his selection is in no real sense part of the manner of holding the election. This does not depend upon the scheme by which candidates are put forward. Whether the candidate be offered through primary, or convention, or petition, or request of a few, or as the result of his own unsupported ambition, does not directly affect the manner of holding the election. Birth must precede, but it is no part of either funeral or apotheosis.

Many things are prerequisites to elections or may affect their outcome,—voters, education, means of transportation, health, public discussion, immigration, private animosities, even the face and figure of the candidate; but authority to regulate the manner of holding them gives no right to control any of these. It is settled, e.g., that the power to regulate interstate and foreign commerce does not reach whatever is essential thereto. Without agriculture, manufacturing, mining, etc., commerce could not exist; but this fact does not suffice to subject them to the control of Congress. Kidd v. Pearson, 128 U. S. 1, 32 L. ed. 346, 2 Inters. Com. Rep. 232, 9 Sup. Ct. Rep. 6.

Election of Senators by state legislatures presupposed selection of their members by the people; but it would, hardly be argued that therefore Congress could regulate such selection. In the Constitution Convention of 1787, when replying to the suggestion that state legislatures should have uncontrolled power over elections of members of Congress, Mr. Madison said: 'It seems as improper in principle, though it might be less inconvenient in practice, to give to the state legislatures this great authority over the election of the representatives of the people in the general legislature, as it would be to give to the latter a like power over the election of their representatives in the state legislatures.' Supplement to Elliot's Debates, vol. 5, p. 402.

We cannot conclude that authority to control party primaries or conventions for designating candidates was bestowed on Congress by the grant of power to regulate the manner of holding elections. The fair intendment of the words does not extend so far; the framers of the Constitution did not ascribe to them any such meaning. Nor is this control necessary in order to effectuate the power expressly granted. On the other hand, its exercise would interfere with purely domestic affairs of the state, and infringe upon liberties reserved to the people."

In that case, the Government had argued that, independent of the provisions of the Constitution which have been quoted as to the supervisory power of Congress over the times, places and manner of holding "elections," there was an *implied* power in the Federal Government to regulate any activity of the citizen, which had any reference to the election of federal officers, but the Supreme Court denied any such implied power and, if it had not done so, there would have been little liberty left to the states in a matter so vital to their welfare.

There is a clear distinction between the machinery of "elections" from the registration of the voter and the final casting of the ballot, over which Congress has undoubtedly this supervisory power, and the collateral and ancillary activities of citizens in selecting their candidates and in conducting their political campaigns.

To argue that the Federal Government has either an express or implied power to regulate all activities of the citizen, which have any relation to elections, is to assert that the Federal Government could substantially destroy the political activities of the citizens. Thus it could regulate the character of political campaigns and the machinery of party government, and this would be a most dangerous extension of federal power, of which no man could see the end. For example, Congress could require primaries as against the wish of a State, or could require conventions; or it could restrict candidates or define issues. Where would be the limit of such a power?

However, it is useless to discuss a matter upon which the final arbiter, the Supreme Court, has authoritatively spoken. The conduct of political campaigns and, incidentally, the conduct of primary elections, is a matter beyond the delegated power of the Federal Government and this conclusion accords with the intentions of those who framed the great charter of our government.

The pertinency of this discussion to the current controversy, which has grown out of the Pennsylvania and Illinois primary elections, is obvious. If the Federal Government has no power to legislate with reference to the primaries in Pennsylvania and Illinois, then it is equally without power to reject the deliberate choice of those states, by reason of any alleged irregularities in such primaries.

To nullify the action of these sovereign states, by reason

of the actions of irresponsible individuals over which the Federal Government has no supervisory power, would, in effect, be a *coup d'état,* which would radically change our form of government and lead to deplorable and incalculable consequences.

The author recognizes that it is possible to over-estimate the importance of these subtle changes in our form of Government. Nevertheless, if the Senate should, as is now threatened, nullify the action of the States of Pennsylvania or Illinois by denying Mr. Vare and Mr. Smith the seats to which they have been elected, the world will continue to go round and the Government will continue to function, for the Constitution has survived all the subtle changes to which from time to time it has been subject. Its "cloud-capped towers" are not likely to fall into cureless ruin.

This is true, but it is also true that, if such a precedent shall at this late day become part of the great unwritten law of our form of Government, to which from time to time the written law conforms, then the rights of the States will no longer be the same as they were prior to this fatal wound.

Once again in our history, the serious doubt will be suggested to thoughtful men whether a written constitution can be maintained in its full vigor. Written and unwritten constitution are alike subject to the law of change and, while no one need attack the changes which are brought about through the method of amendment provided in the Constitution, yet the modifications, which are due to the changing spirit of the people, or the insidious attacks of parties and factions, may well give the lover of constitutional liberty cause for doubt as to the lasting efficacy of a written constitution.

May it not be said of written, as of unwritten constitutions, that "the best of this kind are but shadows?"

The form too often survives the substance of the faith.

The American people can, in this crisis, prophetically recall the sagacious words of Washington in his Farewell Address, when, speaking as an "old and affectionate friend," he said:

"It is of infinite moment that you should properly estimate the immense value of your national Union to your collective and individual happiness. . . . Towards the preservation of your government, and the permanency of your present happy state, it is requisite, not only that you steadily discountenance irregular oppositions to its acknowledged authority, but also that you resist with care the spirit of innovation upon its principles, however specious the pretexts. *One method of assault may be to effect, in the forms of the Constitution, alterations which will impair the energy of the system, and thus to undermine what cannot be directly overthrown.*"

APPENDICES

APPENDIX A

THE PARLIAMENTARY PRECEDENTS IN ENGLAND AND THE COLONIES

LET us now consider what events the framers had in mind in the language used by them. The present Chief Justice of the United States well said in a very recent case:

> "The language of the Constitution cannot be interpreted safely except by reference to the common law and to British institutions as they were when the instrument was formed and adopted. The statesmen and lawyers of the Convention, who submitted it to the ratification of the conventions of the thirteen states, were born and brought up in the atmosphere of the common law, and thought and spoke in its vocabulary. They were familiar with other forms of government, recent and ancient, and indicated in their discussions earnest study and consideration of many of them, but when they came to put their conclusions into the form of fundamental law, in a compact draft, they expressed them in terms of the common law, confident that they could be shortly and easily understood."

Mediæval English history records little concerning disputed parliamentary elections. Membership in the House of Lords, generally speaking, was hereditary and always for life. Membership in the House of Commons was elective and was regarded as a burden rather than a privilege. The greatest difficulty was in finding candidates who were willing to serve in the House of Commons. For instance, in 1321, we find the Mayor of Lincoln writing to the Keeper of the Rolls that one of the two elected members who had previously agreed to attend the sessions of the House of Commons, now refused to do so.

In 1323 it was alleged by the Grand Jury of West Derby that one Gentil, when sheriff, had returned two members of the House of Commons without the consent of the County and that he had levied twenty pounds for their wages, when he could have found two men who would have served for ten pounds each. Members of the House of Commons were then paid by their constituents. In 1362 we find the King writing the sheriff that there was great dispute concerning an election and directing him to hold an examination in full County Court as to the question whether the two persons named in the return had been actually elected. At such examination it was found that the two persons named in the return were lieutenants of the sheriff and that they had returned themselves without an election and had levied and retained the wages. The King ordered cancellation of the return and a new election. The County of Rutland elected, in 1404, John Pesax and Thomas Thorpe. The sheriff returned Pesax and William Ondeby. The House of Commons made representation of the facts to the King, who directed the House of Lords to inquire into the matter. The House of Lords found that Thorpe, and not Ondeby, had been elected, and the sheriff was removed from office.

These few instances in mediæval English history serve to illustrate the more general complaint against the returns of sheriffs, and also the important point that the House of Commons had not claimed either the jurisdiction or the power to judge the elections, returns and qualifications of its members. Until the Act of 1406, the sheriffs made the returns to the full Parliament. The King, in or out of Parliament, took direct cognizance of all complaints arising out of the election of members of the House of Commons. After that act, the returns were made to the Court of Chancery, and by the Act of 1410 the Judges of Assize were authorized to inquire into the validity of elections of members of the House of Commons.

The right of the House of Commons to judge of the election of its members appears to have been first distinctly asserted in 1604, with reference to an election from Buckinghamshire. This assertion of the right of the House of Commons is described by Anson (Vol. 1, Law and Custom of the Constitution, pages 169-170), as follows:

"James I, in the proclamation for calling his first Parliament, took upon himself to admonish all persons concerned with the election of knights of shires, that, among other things, they should take express care that no bankrupt or outlaw was elected; he further announced that all returns should be made to the Chancery, and that if such returns were contrary to the tenor of his proclamation, they 'should be rejected as unlawful and insufficient.'

Sir Francis Goodwin, an outlaw, was returned for the County of Bucks. On the return of his election being made, it was refused by the clerk of the Crown on the ground of the outlawry. The clerk issued a new writ on his own authority, and Sir John Fortescue was returned.

The House inquired into the matter, and having examined the clerk of the Crown, resolved that Goodwin was duly elected, and ordered the indenture of his return to be filed in the Crown office.

The Lords first took the matter up, and asked an explanation of the Commons; the Commons refused to discuss the question. A message then came from the Lords that the King desired the two Houses to confer upon the election. The Commons thereupon demanded access to the King, and stated the grounds of their action. The King asserted that returns 'being all made into the Chancery are to be corrected and reformed by that Court only into which they are returned', and he desired the House to hold a conference with the Judges. This, after a long debate, the House determined not to do, but submitted an argumentative memorial to the King, meeting his objections and alleging precedents for the right they claimed. It is noticeable, that of the five precedents set forth, two only are cases of disputed returns, two are cases of disqualified persons being returned, and one a case of a member being returned for two places.

The King was not satisfied with the answer of the House; he still desired a conference between the Commons and the Judges. To this the Commons reluctantly assented; a conference took place before the King and council, and the King in the end admitted the right of the House to be a court of record and judge of returns, though he claimed a corresponding jurisdiction for the Chancery; and he suggested as a compromise, that the elections of Fortescue and Goodwin should both be held void and a new writ issued. This was done, and the right of the Commons was not afterwards questioned, nor that of the Chancery asserted."

From the time of the Restoration to the Grenville Act of 1770, election petitions were determined by the whole House, but that Act provided for the formation of election committees to pass upon contested elections. The Grenville Act was occasioned by the action of the House of Commons in expelling John Wilkes.

Some significant and very pertinent passages from Grenville's great speech in the Wilkes' case may be profitably quoted : *

"By the fundamental principles of this constitution, the right of judging upon the general propriety or unfitness of their representatives is entrusted with the electors, and when chosen this House can only exclude or expel them for some disability established by the law of the land, or for some specific offence alleged and proved. If it were otherwise, we should in fact elect ourselves, instead of being chosen by our respective constituents. If I had been one of the electors for the county of Middlesex, I should have shown by my vote the opinion which I entertained with regard to the conduct and character of Mr. Wilkes, and to the propriety of choosing him a knight of the shire for that county. I had not only a right, but it would have been my duty to have manifested that opinion. But when he is chosen and returned hither, my duty is widely different. We are now acting in our judicial capacity, and are therefore to found the judgment which we are to give, not upon our wishes and inclinations, not upon our private belief or arbitrary opinions, but upon specific facts alleged and proved according to the established rules and course of our proceedings. When we are to act as judges, we are not to assume the character of legislators, any more than the Court of King's Bench, who were bound to

* The full speech will be found in Appendix B.

reverse Mr. Wilkes's outlawry if they found any irregularity in it, tho' possibly they were convinced in their private opinions, that it would have been more beneficial to the state to have confirmed it. If we depart from this principle, and allow to ourselves a latitude of judging in questions of this nature, if we are to admit those whom we think most improper, to what lengths will not this doctrine carry us? There never was a parliament chosen, into which there were not some persons elected whom the greater part of the House thought unworthy of that honour. I speak of former parliaments, and it becomes us to be careful that posterity should not speak still worse of us."

Later, in the course of this noble speech, he said:

"Let not your prejudices, let not your just resentments against the conduct and character of the man, who is now the object of our deliberation, prevail upon you to ground any part of your proceedings upon such destructive and fatal principles. Consider that precedents of this nature are generally begun in the first instance against the odious and the guilty, but when once established, are easily applied to and made use of against the meritorious and the innocent; that the most eminent and best deserving members of the state, under the colour of such an example, by one arbitrary and discretionary vote of one House of Parliament (the worst species of ostracism) may be excluded from the public councils, cut off and proscribed from the rights of every subject of the realm, not for a term of years alone, but for ever; that a claim of this nature would be to assume to the majority of this House alone, the powers of the whole legislature; for nothing short of their united voice, declared by an act of parliament, has hitherto pretended to exercise such a general discretion of punishing, contrary to the usual forms of law, and of enacting such a perpetual incapacity upon any individual. There are indeed some instances of the latter kind in our statute books, but even there they have been frequently animadverted upon, and heavily censured as acts of violence and injustice, and breaches of the constitution. Let us remember the well known observation of the learned and sensible author of *'L'Esprit des Lois'*,* who states it as one of the excellencies of the English Constitution, of which he was a professed admirer, 'that the judicial power is separated from the legislative'; and tells us 'that there would be no liberty if they were blended together, that the power over the life and liberty of the citizens would then be arbitrary; for the judge would be the legislator'. Shall we, then, who are the immediate delegated guardians of that liberty and constitution, shall we set the wicked example, and attempt to violate them to gratify our passions or our prejudices?"

The Grenville Act transferred the decision of disputed returns from the whole House to a committee, selected by lot from a list of 49 members, from which list the petitioner and the sitting member struck off names alternatively until the number was reduced to 13. No appeal lay to the House, whose privileges in this respect were henceforth limited by the operation of the statute. This latter procedure continued until 1868, when the Parliamentary Elections Act of that year returned to the earlier procedure of making the courts the judges of the election and returns of members of the House of Commons. However, we are not now concerned with the procedure followed by the House of Commons after the Constitutional Convention of 1787.

Of greater pertinence are the precedents in the Colonies prior to the Revolution.

The proposed New York Charter of Liberties in 1684 contained a provision giving the Governor and the Assembly jurisdiction and power to judge of the elections and qualifications of members of the Assembly, but at a meeting of His Majesty's Privy Council the provision was disapproved for the reason that "it may be inconvenient and is not practiced in some other plantations." Notwithstanding the opinion of the Privy Council, it seems to be clear that practically all of the other thirteen colonies followed the practice of the House of Commons of the time in permitting the legislatures to be the judges of the election, returns and qualifications of their members.

* Montesquieu.

Thus, Massachusetts, by the very law which authorized the sending of deputies to the General Court, or Assembly, gave them power to hear and determine among themselves any differences which might arise as to the election of any of their members. The General Court, or Assembly, of Plymouth reserved to itself the power of rejecting unfit deputies, and New Hampshire, nearly a century afterwards, gave to the town officers the power of settling disputes in regard to elections; in the event of their failure to agree, the decision was left to the lower house of the Assembly. The Hartford Constitution conferred upon the General Assembly the power of judging of their own elections, and it seems that when the general management of elections was delegated to a Grand Committee of both houses in Rhode Island, the decision over contests and qualifications of members was included.

The laws of 1682 of Pennsylvania recognized the right of both houses of the legislature to judge of the election of their own members, although when the upper house later ceased to be an elective body, its power to judge the election of its members was necessarily abolished.

The method of trying a contested election was by scrutiny of the votes cast for the purpose of correcting any error that might exist in the poll, and in 1737 the New York Legislature spent a month in making such a scrutiny. Virginia recognized the English method of contest by petition of the defeated candidate, as well as the scrutiny before the House of Burgesses.

It is interesting and instructive to note in this connection that Virginia had an experience somewhat similar to that of England in the case of John Wilkes. John Breckinridge was about to set out from home for his third year at college, when he was elected to represent his county in the House of Delegates. This was in the autumn of 1780, when he was only nineteen years of age. He had made no canvass and was, in no true sense, a candidate. His election was the result of one of those silent movements when men are brought, under the pressure of events, to select those who can best represent them, without regard to the claims of office-seekers. The House of Delegates refused Breckinridge his seat on account of his youth, feeling, no doubt, that the choice was both unprecedented and out of place in a time so full of danger and demanding the most far-sighted counsels. But the hardy frontiersmen had not made their choice without being convinced of its wisdom and promptly reëlected Mr. Breckinridge. The House of Delegates again refused him a seat and again the electors cast their ballots as before. This time the election was acquiesced in by the House of Delegates, and the young student left his academy pursuits in one part of the town and took his seat in the Legislature at the other end of the town.

The laws of North and South Carolina required the sheriffs to attend the legislatures for the first three days and the first two days, respectively, of their sitting, for the "purpose of giving information in event of a contest and also of showing the Assembly a list of the votes cast for each person." Georgia required a scrutiny, if demanded by any member of the Legislature, and returning officers of the elections were required to attend under penalty of a fine of fifty pounds, for the purpose of giving information concerning any question arising as to the election of members.

The power of the legislatures of the various thirteen colonies to judge of the election and qualifications of their members related only to the final election and did not extend to an examination of the regularity of nominations by the people of candidates for election. Nominations were not made by opposing political parties. They were practically a preliminary election for the purpose of reducing the number of eligible candidates by a process of exclusion. Primaries were unknown.

The first definite trace of formal nominations appears in the Hartford Constitution of 1638, in which it was provided that no person could be newly chosen magistrate unless his name had been proposed at the General Court of Assembly in September and voted upon at the regular Court of Elections in the following April. New Haven provided by statute of 1648 that "when any man of what plantation soever, shall be first proposed for magistrate within this jurisdiction, reasonable notice shall be first given to all the plantations of such a purpose or desire, that all the freemen may duly consider and inform themselves." The Connecticut Charter continued the Hartford practice and candidates were nominated by "papers," in order to be voted upon in the election in May.

Massachusetts developed a system of nominations similar in many respects to that of Connecticut, while the series of fundamental constitutions, drawn up in 1683 for East Jersey, combined in a singular manner the Greek idea of election by means of lot and the more modern idea of election by free choice of the voters. It was provided that the names of all persons in each county eligible for the Legislature should be written on a piece of parchment and placed in a box. A boy, under twelve years of age, was required to draw out 50 of the names. These were then placed in a second box and 25 of them were drawn out by the boy and the remaining names constituted the nominators, who selected from their number the requisite number of candidates to be elected by the vote of the people. This system of nomination by "lot and suffrage" is similar to that proposed by the philosopher Harrington, in his "Oceana," who used the lot to determine who should propose the candidates, and the suffrage to decide which of the number proposed should be elected.

In Georgia the Act of 1761 refers to "a person presented or presenting himself as a candidate," and suggests that the English system of nomination by petition was in vogue.

Thus, when the Convention of 1787 framed the Constitution of the United States and the state conventions ratified it, the distinction between elections and nominations was well recognized. When the Seventeenth Amendment was ratified, party campaigns and nominations had become the rule in many states for all elective officers in both federal and state government.

It is significant that neither the original Constitution nor the Seventeenth Amendment gave the federal government any control over nominations of party campaigns. The views of the Senate Committee in the case of Senator Stephenson, already referred to, who had been charged with excessive expenditures in a party primary, disclaimed the right of the Senate to expel a Senator on that ground. The same view was later adopted and followed by the Senate in the more recent case of Senator Newberry, who was given his seat.

APPENDIX B

SPEECH

OF GEORGE GRENVILLE

ON THE

MOTION FOR EXPELLING MR. WILKES
Friday, February 3, 1769

Motion made by Lord Barrington, and seconded by Mr. Rigby

THAT John Wilkes, Esq; a member of this House, who hath at the Bar of this House confessed himself to be the Author and Publisher of what this House has resolved to be an insolent, scandalous, and seditious Libel, and who has been convicted in the Court of King's Bench, of having Printed and Published a Seditious Libel, and three obscene and impious Libels, and by the judgment of the said Court has been sentenced to undergo twenty-two Months Imprisonment, and is now in Execution under the said Judgment, be expelled this House.

Mr. Speaker,

I have endeavoured to form my judgment with regard to this Question, which was not unexpected, upon the fullest and most impartial consideration; and having done so, I do not think myself obliged to make the least apology to any individual, or body of men whatsoever, for the opinion which I shall deliver upon this subject.

I should indeed have wished that I could with propriety have declined delivering my sentiments concerning it, because I am thoroughly sensible that whatever my opinion shall be, it will be liable to great misconstructions and misrepresentations, both within these walls and without doors. If I give my vote for the motion as it was made to you, it will be said, that I do it from a cruel unrelenting disposition, to gratify a private and personal resentment for the abuse Mr. Wilkes has so liberally thrown upon me, and for that purpose under the mask of zeal for the cause of God and of the King, to persevere in loading an unhappy man, who, it has been frequently said in this House, has been already too severely oppressed by my means, or at least with my concurrence; or it would perhaps be attributed, especially after the temperate conduct which I have endeavoured to hold during this session, to an abject flattery to power, with the mean paltry view of obtaining court favour. On the other hand, if I give my vote against the expulsion of Mr. Wilkes, I shall be charged with levity and inconsistency, with changing my opinions as it may best suit my situation either in or out of office, with adopting new principles from new habitudes and connections, and with a factious design of courting popularity, and distressing all legal government, by supporting and protecting a man, whose behaviour I had so repeatedly and so heavily censured. If I know my own failings, revenge and cruelty are among the vices to which I am least inclined; and if I may trust to the reproaches thrown out against me by my enemies, I have been often accused of obstinacy and inflexibility of temper, but seldom or never I think with being too much disposed to alter my opinions according to the will of others, or to fail along the tide of popular prejudice. I should flatter myself therefore, that the charge of sacrificing principles to court favour or popular applause, could not with justice be applied to me, notwithstanding which I will again freely own, that I should have wished for many reasons not to have been under the necessity of deciding upon this Question, either one way or the other. But as it has been proposed to you, I think it would be a base and unworthy conduct meanly to hide my head or to run away from the difficulty. On the contrary, it is the duty of every honest man, if he is convinced that the judgment which he has formed is a right one, to declare it publicly in his place, to abide by it, and boldly to face any difficulties which may encounter it. I am under no restraint either from this or that side of the House, I know and feel my own independence on both, and while I continue here, I will exert it, and upon this occasion execute an office greater than any which the wildest applause of the multitude can give, or than the King himself can bestow, greater than the office of First Commissioner of the Treasury, or either of the Secretaries of State: the honourable and noble office of speaking the truth, and of doing impartial justice. I will not palliate this man's offences, or try to move your compassion: for that would be to appeal to your weakness against your judgment, much less will I inveigh against him in bitter terms, and strive to excite your indignation: for instead of your weakness I should then apply to your wicked passions. With these sentiments I shall proceed to the immediate examination of the Question before you. And in the first place, I cannot agree with those who have urged in behalf of Mr. Wilkes, that this motion ought not to be complied with, because he is already the most unhappy, as well as the most oppressed and injured man that this age has seen: he is indeed unhappy, because he is guilty, and guilt must ever produce unhappiness; but in other respects, considering his repeated offences, he has certainly been more fortunate, than his most sanguine wishes could have expected. I mean not to enter into the detail of all that has happened to him, it would carry me too far, but to justify what I have said, let me ask a few questions. When he wrote that seditious libel against the King and both Houses of Parliament, could he foresee that he should be taken up by a General Warrant, against the declared opinion and desire of the two Secretaries of State, who repeatedly proposed to have his name inserted in the warrant of apprehension, but were over-ruled by the lawyers and clerks of the office, who insisted they could not depart from the long established precedents and course of proceedings. Could Mr. Wilkes foresee, that after an hundred years practice, under the eye of the greatest lawyers, before the supreme courts of justice, without being ever questioned in one single instance, that this irregularity and illegality would be first found out in his case, and afterwards adopted by the voice and clamour of the people upon the occasion of his apprehension? Had he been tried and convicted without this irregularity, what would have been his situation, and where his popularity and the liberal support which he has met with? What would have become of the large damages which he has already obtained by this means or the immense sums which he now sues for, and on which he places his last dependance? Are these the proofs that he has been the most unfortunate, or is it more true that he has been the most oppressed and injured man this age has seen. Dr. Shebbeare was taken up by a General Warrant from the Secretary of State, dated 12 January, 1758, conceived word for word in the same terms, for writing the sixth letter to the people of England on the progress of national ruin, in which is shewn, that the present grandeur of France and calamities of this nation are owing to the influence of Hanover on the councils of England. Under this General Warrant all his papers were seized as in the case of Mr. Wilkes, and he was prosecuted for this offence by Mr. Pratt, then Attorney General, now Lord Chancellor of Great Britain. He was tried and convicted of it on the 17th of May, and on the 28th of November following he was sentenced to be fined, to stand in the pillory, to be imprisoned for three years, and then to give security for his good behavior for seven years. The prosecution against Mr. Wilkes was directed by the unanimous address of both Houses of Parliament. He was tried and convicted by a favourable jury, for a libel certainly not less seditious or criminal than Dr. Shebbeare's. He was sentenced to be fined five hundred pounds, and to be imprisoned for one year instead of three years, to give security for his good behaviour for seven years, and the ignominious part of the punishment was wholly remitted. He was tried and convicted likewise for being the author and publisher of the three obscene and impious libels, upon a prosecution directed in consequence of an address from the House of Lords, for which he received exactly the same sentence as for the former offence, including the two months imprisonment, which he had suffered before judgment was given. Was he for either of these offences, or indeed for all of them taken together, so severely dealt with as Dr. Shebbeare for one alone. I do not go any further back, tho' a multitude of similar instances, and some more severe even than that of Dr. Shebbeare might be produced within these last

forty or fifty years.   What I have already mentioned seems
to me fully sufficient to shew, that Mr. Wilkes is not entitled
to any extraordinary plea of his having been the object of
extraordinary severity during the course of the former proceedings.   But, though not to favour, yet he is most certainly
entitled to that justice which is due to every man, and which
we ought to be more particularly careful to preserve, in an
influence where passion and prejudice may both concur in
the violation of it.   These are principles which no one will
dispute with me, and in consequence of them, after having
thoroughly considered the charge contained in your Question,
and the arguments urged in support of it, I am clearly of
opinion, that I ought not to give my assent to the proposition
which has been made to you; because if I did, I should thereby
commit a capital injustice.   I am sensible that the expression is
a strong one, and that it is incumbent upon me to shew my
reasons for applying it to the motion now under your consideration, which I shall endeavour to do as fully and as
satisfactorily as I am able.

I perfectly agree with the gentleman who has told you that
this House has a right to enquire into the conduct of its members, and that they have exercised that right in a great variety
of instances, in which they have tried, censured and expelled
them according to the established course of our proceedings,
and the law of Parliament.   Let us examine the proposition
now before you by this rule, and we shall then be able to judge,
whether it is conformable to the usage and law of parliament,
to the practice of any other court of justice in the kingdom,
or to the unalterable principles of natural equity, or whether
it is a new and dangerous mode of proceedings, unsupported
by any precedent or example in the Journals of Parliament,
or the records of any other court, calculated merely to serve a
present purpose, and as such, well deserving the term which I
gave to it of a capital injustice.   The charge contained in this
motion consists of four articles, each of which it has been contended is sufficient singly to justify the conclusion drawn from
them all put together, that Mr. Wilkes ought to be expelled.
Upon this complicated charge, the House is now called upon

to give a judgment for or against the question. It is a well known and undeniable rule in this House, founded in common sense, that, whenever a question, even of the most trivial nature, is complicated, and contains different branches, every individual Member, has an indubitable right to have the question separated, that he may not be obliged to approve or disapprove in the lump, but that every part of the proposition should stand or fall abstractedly upon its own merits. I need not shew the propriety and the absolute necessity for this; it is so self evident, that every argument I could urge in support of it would only weaken it. And surely if it holds good in all cases where we act only in a deliberative capacity, it will not be contended, that it is less true, or less necessary, when we are to exercise our judicial powers, when we are to censure and to punish, and to affect not only the rights of our own member, but the franchises of those who sent him hither as their representative. I may safely challenge the gentlemen, the most knowing in the Journals of this House, to produce a single precedent of a similar nature. And if none shall be produced, as I am convinced there cannot, am I not founded in saying, that this is a new attempt, unsupported by law and usage of parliament.

But this mode of proceeding is not only new and unprecedented, it is likewise dangerous and unjust. For the proof of it, let me recall to your minds what has passed in the course of this debate; one very learned and worthy gentleman who spoke early, declared, that he gave his consent to this motion for expulsion, upon that article of the charge alone, which relates to the three obscene and impious libels, disavowing, in the most direct terms, all the other articles, because he thought, that the libel relative to Lord Weymouth's letter was not properly and regularly brought before us, and that Mr. Wilkes, having been already expelled by a former parliament, for the seditious libel of the North Briton, ought not to be punished and expelled a second time by a subsequent parliament for the same offence. His argument was, that the former House of Commons, having vindicated the honour of the King and of Parliament, he hoped this House would not shew less zeal to vindicate the cause of God and of Religion. He spoke with a becoming zeal and indignation, raised, as he told us, by having read some of the wicked and impious expressions contained in the Record now upon your table. His opinions (which were soon after followed by another learned gentleman who adopted the same train of reasoning) joined to the serious manner in which he delivered them, seemed to make great impression upon the House, and tho' I differ with him in his conclusion, yet I agree with him in his principles, and was glad to see this offence treated as it ought to be. For, if we treat it with mirth and levity, we in some measure justify the libel itself by our conduct, and share the guilt of the author. On the other hand, what were the arguments of the two noble lords, who spoke lately for the expulsion? They agreed indeed with the learned gentlemen in the conclusion, but differed widely in the premises with regard to the articles of the charge on which they founded their judgment. They both disclaimed the article of the three obscene and impious libels as any ground for this proceeding. They expressed their disapprobation of the manner in which the copy of them was obtained from Mr. Wilkes's servant, and their doubts with regard to his intention to publish them. One of them therefore desired to draw a veil over that part of the charge, that it might no more be mentioned, and the other wished to bury the whole of that transaction in oblivion. The first, waving the rest of the charge, grounded his assent to the motion upon the seditious libel of the North Briton; the latter, if I mistake not, upon the libel against Lord Weymouth. These sentiments likewise seemed to meet with great approbation from many of your members. Another gentleman, who is very conversant in the Journals of the House, and could not therefore but be sensible both of the novelty and danger of this proceeding upon such an accumulated and complicated charge, thought it necessary to take a different ground. He seemed to wave the criminal parts of the charge, but insisted strongly upon Mr. Wilkes's incapacity of continuing a member of Parliament, arising from his imprisonment, which the House had declared to be no case of privilege, and from which they could not therefore discharge him.

I have stated these arguments, and I appeal to the House, whether I have misrepresented them. I might in the same manner go thro' the rest of this debate; I think not above two gentlemen, who have spoken together, have agreed in assigning the same offence as the proper ground for this expulsion. It is impossible to form any judgment concerning the sentiments of those who have not spoken, except from those who have, and from the approbation which has been given to what they declared. If I am to judge from thence, I should imagine, that the opinions of those who concur in this question of expulsion, are almost equally divided among the several branches of the charge contained in it; but however that may be, it is undeniably true, that great numbers of gentlemen approve of some parts of the charge, and disapprove of others, and so, vice versa. What then may be the consequence of blending the whole of this matter together? Is it not evident, that by this unworthy artifice, Mr. Wilkes may be expelled, although three parts in four of those who expell him should have declared against his expulsion upon every one of the articles contained in this charge. Would not this severe punishment be inflicted upon him, in that case, by a minority, against the sense and judgment of a great majority of this House? To explain this in a manner obvious to the apprehension of every gentleman who hears me, let me suppose, that an indictment were framed, consisting of four distinct offences, each inferring the penalty of death; charging for example that the prisoner on the first of May had committed treason, on the first of June murder, on the first of July robbery, and on the first of August forgery. Let me suppose any court of judicature in the Kingdom ignorant and wicked enough to admit of, and to try the prisoner upon such a complicated indictment, notwithstanding any objection he could make to it. Might he not be found guilty of each of these offences by three different jurymen, and declared innocent by nine, and would he not in fact by this contrivance be condemned to death by three, although acquitted by nine? What would mankind, what would you yourselves say of such a sentence so obtained? Would you not think the term of capital injustice too soft an expression? Would you not call it the worst of murders, a murder under the colour of law and justice? The punishment would indeed be different, because the offences are so, but the mode of proceeding on the present occasion is exactly the same and equally inconsistent with the law and usage of parliament, with the practice of every court of judicature in any civilized country, and with the unalterable principles of natural equity. But I will restrain my expressions, and leave this part of the Question to your own feelings, which I am persuaded will enforce it more strongly than any arguments of mine.

I have hitherto taken the whole of this complicated charge together, and have shown the dangerous consequences resulting from it; I will now unravel the web, and consider the different parts of it separately and distinctly. The first which presents itself is the libel relative to Lord Weymouth's letter, which has been new christened for this special purpose. It was complained of in the other House as a breach of privilege, and as a gross and impudent libel, which it certainly is, against a peer of the realm, and one of his Majesty's principal secretaries of State. But when it appeared to be written by Mr. Wilkes, it was to change its name and its nature. The particular complaint and all mention of the noble Lord concerned in it was to be dropped, and it became at once a matter of sedition against the State. With what view was this alteration made? Why did not the House of Lords address the King, to have it prosecuted by the Attorney General, in the same manner as was done with regard to the three obscene and impious libels which were written by the same person then a member of this House, and were likewise complained of as a breach of privilege against a peer of parliament? What was the motive for this difference of proceeding in the other House, on two offences of the same nature against the same person? It was not out of regard to us and to our privileges, for they well knew, that we had joined with them in a solemn declaration, that in this case there was no privilege, and they themselves had proceeded in consequence of it against this very man then a member of Parliament, for a similar offence, without communicating it to the House of Commons. Can any reason be assigned for this, except a desire in their Lordships to shift the jurisdiction, and instead of sending it to the courts of law, where libels against ministers have hitherto always been tried, to transmit it to us to be punished, contrary to all precedent and example, by an extraordinary extension of our judicature? And will this House, whose peculiar duty it is to watch over and to guard the laws of the land from all encroachments, and who have looked with the most jealous eye upon every act which has the least tendency to exempt the peers of the realm, and their causes from that jurisdiction which is common to all, will this House, I say, lend its name to such an evasion, and extend its judicature for such a purpose? Shall we take upon ourselves so odious an office, and answer such a demand at sight, with no other view, than to save their Lordships the difficulty and obloquy which is the usual consequence of these prosecutions? If this attempt should succeed, and so easy and summary a method should be marked out for the punishment of those who shall libel ministers of State, this probably will not be the last application which we shall receive of this nature. We have enough to do, too much I fear, to maintain our own authority and dignity unimpeached, and surely the other House has sufficient power in themselves, with the assistance of the courts of law, to vindicate their members from every insult.

The next article is that of the seditious libel the North Briton, for which, the author and publisher was deservedly prosecuted, tried and convicted five years ago, in consequence of the unanimous address of both Houses of Parliament. He was likewise expelled by the last House of Commons for the indignity offered to them by one of their own members, of which they were the only judges, and which they alone could punish; a case so widely different from that of a libel on any particular person or minister of state, that it is quite unnecessary to do more than to mark it out to your observation. For this libel of the North Briton Mr. Wilkes has been sentenced, and is now undergoing the punishment, inflicted on him by Law. He has likewise been punished by expulsion from the former House of Commons for the particular offence committed against them. There is not a rule more sacred in the jurisprudence of this country, than that a man once acquitted or condemned, shall not be tried or punished again by the same judicature for the same offence. How many notorious criminals daily escape by the strict observance of this rule, and yet the principle of it is so salutary, and so deeply rooted in the minds of men, that no one dares to set his face against it, and to avow an intention to break through it. It was but a few days ago that I spoke and voted to restrain Mr. Wilkes from entering into the greater part of his petition, because the subject matter of his complaint had been fully heard, and the parties to it duly acquitted by the last House of Commons. The House, after long debate, adopted the reasoning, and Mr. Wilkes was restrained accordingly.

And shall I, within the little space of a few days, forget every argument which I then used against him, and declare without shame that the same rule of law, which was conclusive when urged in behalf of his adversaries, should in the same cause be of no avail when pleaded in his favour. Is this that consistency upon which I, and those who hear me, are to value ourselves? I have not taken up that sacred principle so lightly, nor will I so wantonly depart from it. Permit me to give you an instance of it. Many years ago, a proposition was made to allow of a revision of the sentence of a court martial. The Question was solemnly argued. I then sat at the treasury board with a minister for whom I had the highest personal regard and respect; and yet in opposition to him, and to the sentiments of those, with whom I was connected by the nearest ties both of blood and friendship, I repeatedly voted and spoke against that revision, in conjunction with a noble person, who then sat at the same board with me, and an honourable gentleman, an officer of the army, who afterwards, held the office of one of his Majesty's Principal Secretaries of State, who now hears me, and to whom I appeal for the truth of what I have said upon this subject. Is not this the revision of a sentence given in a former parliament in order to encrease it? And if this motion for the expulsion of Mr. Wilkes, as grounded upon that offence, shall prevail, will he not be twice expelled and twice punished for one crime by the same judicature, in direct violation of that salutary principle, to the truth of which we ourselves have so lately assented.

The third article, contained in the charge is for Printing and Publishing three impious and obscene Libels, under the title of the Essay upon Woman; I trust that none who hear me, I am sure that no one who knows me will believe, that I mean to palliate that crime, or the seditious and dangerous Libel which I have just now mentioned. I will go further, I cannot agree with those who think, that the papers relative to it were obtain'd by those who prosecuted him in any undue or improper manner. The contrary has appeared by Mr. Wilkes's own evidence a few days ago. That Prosecution was begun in another place, and I had nothing to do with it; but in justice to those who were concerned, I must say, that there was not the least foundation for all that calumny that has been propagated with regard to the manner of obtaining them, for the truth of which I appeal to the examination which the House has so lately made on Mr. Wilkes's petition upon that subject. I must therefore freely declare, that this observation has no weight with me. The other part of the objection is founded upon the evidence given at your Bar, that Mr. Wilkes had directed only 12 copies of them to be printed, and strictly ordered, that they should all be delivered into his own hands, from whence it is urged, that he had no intention to publish them at large. This may be indeed a circumstance of alleviation which I am the more authorised to say, as I am informed it was mentioned by the learned judge, in mitigation of the sentence given against him in the Court of King's Bench. But the strongest plea in his defence upon this head is, that the crime was committed five years ago, that the law has already punished it, that the last House of Commons, though they were not ignorant of it when they proceeded against him, and certainly were not partial to him, yet, as they were not particularly concerned in it, did not think it right for them to interfere in it. It might therefore be thought a hardship to him to let it pass unnoticed by them, and many years after to transfer it to another parliament, and to reserve it in so unusual a manner for a fresh censure.

The last article of this complicated charge is, that Mr. Wilkes has been sentenced by the judgment of the court of King's Bench to undergo twenty-two months imprisonment, and that he is now in execution under that judgment. This circumstance has been principally relied upon and enforced by a gentleman, who has labour'd very strongly to prove that, as Mr. Wilkes is thereby disabled from taking his seat, and doing his duty for sixteen months to come, this disability alone is a proper and sufficient ground to justify the proposition which has been made to you for expelling him. You have been told very truly, that his constituents have the clearest and most undeniable right to the attendance of their representatives in parliament, that there is no privilege which we are or ought to be so tender of as to free our members from the least restraint, which may prevent or even interrupt them in the exercise of this duty, that this consideration is of such infinite moment, that the usual course of justice in all civil cases is to give way to it and be suspended, in order to preserve the right of our constituents from being violated in the smallest degree: that we have already declared, that Mr. Wilkes is not entitled by privilege of parliament to be discharged from his imprisonment, and that we have no other method to enforce the attendance of our member: that under these circumstances he would for a long time to come be utterly disabled from performing that duty which he owes to his constituents, unless the king should be pleased to pardon him, which would in effect be leaving to the option of the crown to determine, whether one of our members should or should not take his seat in this House.

I entirely concur with the general positions which have been laid down as the foundation of this argument, but I differ extremely in the consequences which have been drawn from it, and think that I can shew by a demonstration, that by the law and constant usage of parliament, the inability of attending his duty for the space of a year or two has never been deemed a sufficient reason for the expulsion of a member. I say his inability, for his imprisonment has justly been stated, not as a fresh crime, but as an inability in him to attend, and in the

House to reclaim him. The proposition therefore is, that whenever a member is restrained from doing his duty here, and that the House cannot compel his attendance without the immediate interposition and consent of the Crown, in all such cases the House is bound by the law and practice of parliament to proceed to an expulsion of the member so disabled.

Let us see how far this doctrine is warranted by former precedents. Not one has been produced in support of it. On the contrary, need I put that gentleman in mind of a multitude of examples, many of which have happened in our own time, which prove the very reverse of it. Does he not remember the case of Lord Barrymore and Sir John Douglas, both of them members of this House, who were imprisoned upon the suspension of the Habeas Corpus Act for a longer period of time than Mr. Wilkes, and who could not be deliver'd from that imprisonment without the interposition and consent of the Crown? Many cases of a similar nature must be fresh in the memory of us all, but there is one which I cannot mention without a particular respect and reverence to the person concerned in it. I mean the case of Sir William Wyndham. He was imprisoned in the Tower for upwards of two years, during which time the county which he represented, and the public in general, were deprived of those services for which he was so eminently qualified, and which he performed with so much honour to himself and advantage to them. But though the times were warm and violent, and many wished to get rid of those abilities which they were well acquainted with, yet no man ventured in that or any of the other instances to maintain the doctrine now laid down, that because the parties were restrained from their attendance here by a legal imprisonment, from which this House could not deliver them without the interposition and consent of the Crown, they therefore ought by the law and constitution of Parliament to be expelled.

I am well aware that in these cases it may be said, the parties had not been convicted, that there is therefore a great difference as to the certainty of the crime imputed to them. It is true, and God forbid that I should draw any parallel of that kind, but with regard to the restraint abstracted from the crime, which is made the only foundation of this part of the argument, it is exactly the same as in the present instance. Nor will the consequences stop here, if it should be admitted that this argument is well founded; I am convinced the gentleman who urged it was not aware of them. Would he wish that all those whom the king can by law restrain from their attendance in this House for the space of 15 or 16 months, and who are thereby unable to discharge the duty which they owe to their con-stituents. Would he wish, I say, that they should be all de-clared, ipso facto, incapable of sitting in parliament after that restraint shall be ended; has he forgotten how many officers both in the land and sea service, whilst they were members of this House, were absent for many years together, during the late war? Are there not many in the same situation, who are at this very time actually employed upon military services in our garrisons abroad? Can they leave that duty without the interposition and consent of the Crown: or, if they cannot, will it be contended, that they are disabled from ever returning amongst us, and that their seats are thereby vacated. This doctrine, if true, would prove, that the gentlemen of the Army and of the Navy, who from the nature and condition of the respective services, are at all times liable to this objection, are for that reason not eligible into this House, and would be the strongest argument for an act of parliament declaring their incapacity.

Many other cases might be put of temporary disabilities, even for a longer space of time, which have never been, and I believe never will be deemed proper grounds for an expulsion. I shall not however state them particularly, because those which I have already stated will surely be sufficient to convince the House, that this proposition is directly contrary to the practice, and that it has never been warranted in any one instance by the law and usage of parliament.

But it has been urged, whatever may be the case in point of form, with regard to the several articles contained in this ques-tion, whether taken together as an accumulated and com-plicated charge, or considered separately and distinctly, yet this House must necessarily be the judges, whether any member of their own is or is not a fit person to sit amongst them, and it has been argued, that if the last parliament thought him unfit, the present has certainly an equal right to adjudge that he is so. It has been asked, what merit has he had since that time to recommend him, and to induce the present parliament to think him a properer man to sit amongst them, than he was to sit among their predecessors.

This would indeed be a conclusive argument, if we really had that discretionary power of excluding all those whom we think improper upon which it is founded. But we have no such general authority vested in us, nor is there a single precedent where we have pretended to exercise it. Whenever this House has expelled any member, it has invariably assign'd some particular offence as the reason for such expulsion. By the fundamental principles of this constitution, the right of judging upon the general propriety or unfitness of their representatives is entrusted with the electors, and when chosen, this House can only exclude or expell them for some disability established by the law of the land, or for some specific offence alledged and proved. If it were otherwise, we should in fact elect ourselves, instead of being chosen by our respective constituents. If I had been one of the electors for the county of Middlesex, I should have shown by my vote the opinion which I entertained with regard to the conduct and character of Mr. Wilkes, and to the propriety of choosing him a knight of the shire for that county. I had not only a right, but it would have been my duty to have manifested that opinion. But when he is chosen and returned hither; my duty is widely different. We are now acting in our judicial capacity, and are therefore to found the judgment which we are to give, not upon our wishes and inclinations, not upon our private belief or arbitrary opinions, but upon specific facts alledged and proved according to the established rules and course of our proceedings. When we are to act as judges, we are not to assume the characters of legislators, any more than the Court of King's Bench, who were bound to reverse Mr. Wilkes's outlawry if they found any irregularity in it, tho' possibly they were convinced in their private opinions, that it would have been more beneficial to the state to have confirmed it. If we depart from this principle, and allow to ourselves a latitude of judging in questions of this nature, if we are to admit those whom we think most proper, and to expell those whom we think most improper, to what lengths will not this doctrine carry us? There never was a parliament chosen, into which there were not some persons elected whom the greater part of the House thought unworthy of that honour. I speak of former parliaments, and it becomes us to be careful that posterity should not speak still worse of us.

Let me suppose for a moment, that this were true, to a certain degree even in the present parliament, and that it were carried still farther from party prejudice, or from motives less defensible. This would indeed be the sure means of purging the House effectually from all ill humours within these walls, and of dispersing them at the same time through every corner of the kingdom. But if this summary mode of reasoning was really meant to be adopted, there was certainly no occasion for our sitting four or five days and nights together, to decide a question, which might as well have been determined in so many minutes. I cannot therefore bring myself to think, that any gentleman will avow the proposition to this extent.

But perhaps some may wish to shelter themselves under the other part of the argument, and may contend, that a Man who has been expelled by a former House of Commons cannot, at least in the judgment of those who concurred in that sentence, be deemed a proper person to sit in the present parliament, unless he has some pardon to plead, or some merit to cancel his former offences. They will find upon examination that this doctrine is almost as untenable as the other. Votes of censure, and even commitments by either House of Parliament acting in that capacity only, determine, as it is well known, with the session. There are indeed some instances, where in matters of contempt and refusal to submit to the orders of the House, the proceeding has been taken up again in a following session. But to transfer an expulsion from one parliament to another, and by this means to establish a perpetual incapacity in the party so expelled, which must be the consequence of it, as this objection will hold equally strong in any future parliament as in the present. This I say, would be contrary to all precedent and example, and inconsistent with the spirit of the constitution.

I could cite many precedents to prove the first part of my assertion, but one alone will be sufficient for my purpose, because that is so signal and so memorable in all its circumstances, as to render any confirmation or inforcement of it quite unnecessary. In quoting this precedent, I beg leave to say, that I do not intend to throw any imputation on any person whatsoever. I neither mean to acquit or to condemn those who were parties to it, but merely to state the fact as it appears from your journals and then to submit the result of it to the judgment of those who hear me.

The case I allude to was that of Mr. Walpole, who was afterwards first minister to king George the First and king George the Second for the term of twenty years and upwards. On the 17th of January 1711 he was voted by the House of Commons guilty of a high breach of trust, and notorious corruption, in receiving the sum of 500 guineas, and taking a note for 500 pounds more on account of two contracts made by him when secretary of war, pursuant to a power granted by the lord treasurer, and for this offence he was committed prisoner to the Tower and expelled from the House. He was immediately re-elected, but declared incapable of being chosen during that parliament. However, on the dissolution of it a year and a half afterwards, he was again chosen into the new parliament, was admitted to take his seat without the least question or objection on account of his former expulsion, and continued a Member of the House of Commons in every subsequent parliament till the year 1742, when he was created earl of Orford.

It cannot be denied that the offence was in its nature infamous, and such a one as rendered the person guilty of it unfit to be trusted with the power to give, or to manage the public money. The same party that expelled him, whose enmity was aggravated by his great talents and knowledge of business, continued equally adverse to him, and equally prevalent in the new parliament; but however desirous they were to get rid of him, and however violent upon many other occasions, yet in the very zenith of their power, they did not dare to set up this pretence, or to urge the expulsion of a former parliament, although not two years before, as a sufficient ground for re-expelling or declaring him incapable of sitting in a new parliament. If this could have been attempted, every circumstance concurred to make them wish it. The crime itself was breach of trust, and notorious corruption in a public officer relative to public money, an offence in the eye of parliament certainly not less infamous or less criminal than writing and publishing a seditious libel. Few if any were more obnoxious, or more formidable to them than the gentleman who had been the object of their justice or resentment. The heat of party rage had been pleaded in excuse, if not in justification of many extravagancies on both sides, but they thought this measure beyond the mark of a common violence, and therefore dared not to attempt it.

I have said before, that it was not my intention to approve or to blame the censure then passed upon that extraordinary man. It was the subject of great discussion and altercation at the time. I do not wish to revive past heats. The present are more than sufficient, and all wise and good men should endeavor by justice and moderation to allay them. Let us therefore take it either way. Let us suppose, that he was guilty or innocent of the charge to the utmost extent, and then let us consider how the case will apply to that part of the question which is now before us.

The crime, as it related to a fraud concerning the public revenue, was certainly under the immediate cognizance of this House, and was perhaps punishable in no other manner. They punished it as severely as they could, both by imprisonment and expulsion; the former of which ended in a few months, and the consequences of the latter in a year and a half. If he was guilty of a high breach of trust and notorious corruption, he was certainly very unfit to be invested with the most sacred trust in the kingdom, that of a member of the legislature. Had the Question been asked upon that occasion likewise, what merit he had after his first expulsion to recommend him to the subsequent parliament? The answer must have been, that he had persisted in justifying what he had done, that he had appealed not only to his electors, but to the world at large in more than one printed pamphlet, accusing the House of Commons which had condemned him, of violence and injustice. With all these aggravations, and with every other inducement, what could have protected him, what could have prevented his re-expulsion, but the notoriety and the certainty that such a measure was not consistent with the known law and usage of parliament, even when exerted against a guilty and obnoxious man? This is the state of the argument upon that supposition; but if we take the other part of the alternative, and suppose that he was innocent of the charge, the proposition would be much stronger; we must then consider him in the light of a man expelled by party rage, or on worse motives, not for his crimes but for his merit, not that he was unfit, but that he was too well qualified for the trust reposed in him. What would have been the consequence, if this doctrine of transferring the disability incurred by a former sentence to a subsequent parliament had been then established? The public and this House would have been deprived for ever of those services, which from his knowledge and talents they had a right to expect, and which they so much relied upon, particularly in the important business of the finances of this kingdom, and that gentleman and his family would have been precluded, irreparably precluded, by an unjust judgment, from those great emoluments and high honours which were conferred upon him by two successive kings, as the rewards of his administration. That loss however would have been the misfortune of individuals, but a much heavier, a much more extensive misfortune would have befallen the parliament and the constitution, if so dangerous a precedent had taken place. An easy and effectual plan would have been marked out to exclude from this House for ever, by an unjust vote once passed, any member of it who should be obnoxious to the rage of party, or to the wantonness of power.

Let not your prejudices, let not your just resentments against the conduct and character of the man, who is now the object of our deliberation, prevail upon you to ground any part of your proceedings upon such destructive and fatal principles. Consider that precedents of this nature are generally begun in the first instance against the odious and the guilty, but when once established, are easily applied to and made use of against the meritorious and the innocent : that the most eminent and best deserving members of the state, under the color of such an example, by one arbitrary and discretionary vote of one House of Parliament (the worst species of Ostracism) may be excluded from the public councils, cut off and proscribed from the rights of every subject of the realm, not for a term of years alone, but for ever : that a claim of this nature would be to assume to the majority of this House alone, the powers of the whole legislature; for nothing short of their united voice, declared by an act of parliament, has hitherto pretended to exercise such a general discretion of punishing, contrary to the usual forms of law, and of enacting such a perpetual incapacity upon any individual.

There are indeed some instances of the latter kind in our statute books, but even there they have been frequently animadverted upon, and heavily censured as acts of violence and injustice, and breaches of the constitution. Let us remember the well known observation of the learned and sensible author of "L'Esprit des Loix," who states it as one of the excellencies of the English constitution, of which he was a professed admirer, "that the judicial power is separated from the legislative;" and tells us "that there would be no liberty if they were blended together, that the power over the life and liberty of the citizens would then be arbitrary; for the judge would be the legislator."

Shall we then, who are the immediate delegated guardians of that liberty and constitution, shall we set the wicked example, and attempt to violate them to gratify our passions or our prejudices? And for whom and upon what occasion? Not to preserve the sacred person of sovereign from assassination, or his kingdoms from invasion or rebellion, not to defeat the arbitrary designs of a desperate minister or a despotic court, but to inflict an additional punishment upon a libeller, who appears by the question itself to have been convicted of the greater part of his offences by due course of law, and to be in actual imprisonment at this moment, under a legal sentence pronounced by the supreme court of criminal justice in consequence of that conviction. Can we say, that there are not laws in being, to preserve the reverence due to the magistrate, and to protect the dignity of the crown from scandalous and seditious libels? Are they not sufficient, if temperately and firmly executed, to punish and to deter the most daring from the commission of those offences. If they are, for what purpose is this application? If they are not, can the proposition now made to you be deemed the proper or the effectual method of enforcing them?

This brings me to the only part of the question which I have not yet touched upon; I mean the propriety and wisdom of this measure; supposing even that it were clearly warranted by the law of the land, by the law and usage of parliament, by the spirit of our constitution, and by the general principles of natural justice: the contrary of which I think I have manifestly shown in every one of those particulars. What then are the motives of propriety and wisdom by which we are called upon to come into this extraordinary resolution? I shall probably be told, that it is to check and to restrain the spirit of faction and disorder, to re-establish the credit and authority of government, and to vindicate the honour of this House, by expressing our abhorrence of these offences. No man has been more desirous to attain these necessary purposes than I have been, or will now set his foot farther for the accomplishment of them by all just and legal means, in every instance consistent with the public safety. I have not changed my sentiments relative to Mr. Wilkes, of whom I continue to think exactly in the same manner as I have long done; but, whatever my sentiments are, it cannot be denied, that he is now become an object of popular favour. Nor is that popular favour confined to this capital, or to its neighborhood alone, but is extended to the distant parts of the kingdom. The temper of the people you have been truly told, has on several occasions appeared to be disorderly and licentious, spurning at the laws and at all lawful authority. The difficulties we have to struggle with, arising from the interior condition of this country, from the disobedience of our colonies, and from the state of our foreign affairs, are augmented to such a degree, as to form a very dangerous crisis. The respect and reverence due to the parliament, and the confidence reposed in this House, are visibly diminished.

Under these circumstances does it not behove us to be doubly cautious, not to exceed the strictest bounds of law and of the constitution? Is it not more adviseable, if the case can admit of a doubt, to conciliate the heated minds of men by temper and discretion, than to inflame them by adding fresh fuel to discontent? Our situation, I am sure, demands the firm support of an united people, and their affectionate reliance upon the wisdom of those who govern them. Till that can be restored, at least in some measure, we may look around for order and for obedience in vain. If his Majesty's servants can think that this proceeding is the likely means to restore it, let them, for the sake of this House, whose existence depends upon the good opinion of our constituents, as their happiness does upon us; let them for their own sakes, consult that best guide of all human wisdom, the experience of past times; and where can they consult it more properly than in the history of our own country. There they will find some of the ablest ministers and the most victorious general that any age could boast of, disgraced and overturned in the midst of their success and triumph by a popular clamour of the danger of the church. The reverent incendiary, Dr. Sacheverall, was unwisely prosecuted by this House. He became by that means the favourite and the idol of the people throughout England as much, nay more, than Mr. Wilkes is now. The Queen herself was stopped and insulted in her chair during the trial, with God save Dr. Sacheverell. I heartily wish that no similar insult may have been offered to our present sovereign. The prosecution went on and the ferment encreased. The event verified a famous expression in those days, "that the whigs had wished to roast a parson, and that they had done it at so fierce a fire, that they had burnt themselves," for the ministers were dismissed and the parliament dissolved. The reverend doctor, the mob idol, when he ceased to be a martyr, soon sunk into his original insignificancy, from which that martyrdom alone had raised him.

Mr. Wilkes, apprehensive of the same fate, and thoroughly sensible, that the continuance of his popularity will depend upon your conduct, uses every means in his power to provoke you to some instance of unusual severity. Suppose that you could otherwise have doubted of it, yet his behaviour here at your bar, when called upon to justify himself, is fully sufficient to prove the truth of what I have asserted. If he had intended to deprecate your resentment, and to stop your proceedings against him, he is not so void of parts and understanding, as to have told you in the words he used at the bar (when charged with writing the Libel against lord Weymouth) "that he was only sorry he had not expressed himself upon that subject in stronger terms, and that he certainly would do so whenever a similar occasion should present itself;" nor would he have asked, "whether the precedents quoted by lord Mansfield were not all taken from the Star Chamber." If he had wished to prevent his expulsion, he would have employed other methods to accomplish his purpose; but his object is not to retain his seat in this House, but to stand forth to the deluded people as the victim of your resentment, of your violence and injustice.

This is the advantage which he manifestly seeks to derive from you, and will you be weak enough to give it to him, and to fall into so obvious a snare? What benefit will you gain, or what will he lose, if this motion for his expulsion shall take effect? Whatever talents he has to captivate or to inflame the people without doors, he has none to render him formidable within these walls, or to combat the weighty and powerful arguments which ministers know how to employ. He has holden forth high sounding and magnificent promises of the signal services which he will perform to his country in parliament, and there are many who are ignorant and credulous enough to believe them. Whenever he comes here, I will venture to prophecy that they will be grievously disappointed. That disappointment will be followed by disgust and anger, at their having been so grossly deceived, and will probably turn the tide of popular prejudice. But as soon as he shall be excluded from this House, they will give credit to him for more than he has even promised. They will be persuaded, that every real and imaginary grievance would have been redressed by his patriotic care and influence. If in this situation, any untoward accident, any distress shall befall us, the ferment will be encreased by this circumstance, and the language of an uninformed and misled people will be, "aye, if master Wilkes had been in the House he would have prevented it; they knew that and therefore would not suffer him to come amongst them."

Such will be the reasoning, and such the consequences attending this measure; but they are not the only consequences which ought to be weighed and considered, before you engage in it. Look a little forward to the course of your future proceedings, and see in what difficulties you will involve yourselves.

In the present disposition of the county of Middlesex, you cannot entertain a doubt, but that Mr. Wilkes will be re-elected after his expulsion. You will then probably think yourselves under a necessity of expelling him again, and he will as certainly be again re-elected. What steps can the House then take to put an end to a disgraceful contest, in which their justice is arraigned, and their authority and dignity essentially compromised. You cannot, by the rules of the House, rescind the vote for excluding Mr. Wilkes, in the same session in which it has passed, and I know but two other methods which you can pursue. They have both been the subject of common conversation, and are both almost equally exceptionable.

You may refuse to issue a new writ, and by that means deprive the freeholders of this county of the right of chusing any other representative, possibly for the whole term of the present parliament. There are some examples of this kind in the case of corrupt boroughs, where this House has suspended the issuing a new writ for the remainder of a session, as a punishment upon the voters for the most flagrant bribery; but

I cannot believe, that it will be thought just or advisable to inflict the same punishment during the term of a whole parliament, instead of a single session upon the electors of a great county for no crime, except of rechusing a man whom this House had censured and expelled. If you do not adopt this proceeding, the other alternative will be to bring into this House, as the knight of the shire of Middlesex, a man chosen by a few voters only, in contradiction to the declared sense of a great majority of the freeholders on the face of the poll, upon a supposition, that all the votes of the latter are forfeited and thrown away on account of the expulsion of Mr. Wilkes. If such a proposition shall ever be brought before us, it will then be time enough to enter into a full discussion of it; at present I will only say that, I believe there is no example of such a proceeding, that if it shall appear to be new and unfounded in the law of the land, nay, if any reasonable doubt can be entertained of its legality, the attempt to forfeit the freeholders votes in this manner will be highly alarming and dangerous.

Are these then the proper expedients to check and to restrain the spirit of faction and of disorder, and to bring back the minds of men to a sense of their duty? Can we seriously think they will have that salutary effect? Surely it is time to look forwards and to try other measures. A wise government knows how to enforce with temper, or to conciliate with dignity, but a weak one is odious in the former and contemptible in the latter. How many arguments have we heard from the administration in the course of this session, for conciliating measures towards the subjects in the American colonies, upon questions where the legislative authority of Great Britain was immediately concerned? And is not the same temper, the same spirit of conciliation, at least equally necessary towards the subjects within this kingdom, or is this the only part of the King's dominions where it is not advisable to show it? Let not any gentleman think, that by conciliation I mean a blind and base compliance with popular opinions, contrary to our honour or justice; that would indeed be unworthy of us. I mean by conciliation, a cool and temperate conduct, unmixed with passion, or with prejudice. No man wishes more than I do to stop any excess on either side, or is more ready to resist and tumultuous violence founded upon unreasonable clamour. Such a clamour is no more than a sudden gust of wind which passes by and is forgotten; but when the public discontent is founded in truth and reason; when the sky lowers and hangs heavy all around us, a storm may then arise, which may tear up the constitution by the roots and shake the palace of the King himself.

As for me I have given my opinion, and I have chosen to do it without concert or participation: I can assure the House, that some of my nearest friends did not know the part which I should take. I determined not to tell it, that I might keep myself unengaged and free to change it, if I thought proper, during the course of the debate. I do not mean by this to say, that I came into the House without having formed an opinion; on the contrary, I had weighed and considered it thoroughly, and my judgment upon it is the result of my most serious deliberation. I know not what others may think, or who will act with me upon this occasion. Those who were once my friends may have adopted other ideas and other principles, and even those who still continue to be so, may possibly entertain different sentiments from mine upon this subject. That consideration must not prevent me from doing justice, but God forbid, that they should not exercise the same liberty, and follow their opinions, as I do mine. They know that I have not asked one of them to attend during any part of this business, nor have I desired their concurrence. Many of them sit around me, and I appeal to them for the truth of what I have said.

Thus far then I have discharged my duty, with no other view, but to do that which appears to me most conformable to the ends of justice and of the public welfare, most for the safety and honour of the king and the kingdom. Whilst my little endeavours can contribute but a mite to these great purposes, I will continue to exert them as freely as I have now done; but whenever the violence or corruption of the times, either within or without these walls, will not permit me to follow those dictates uncontrolled, I will leave this place and retire from an assembly, which can no longer be called a free parliament.

Many extravagancies committed by Mr. Wilkes and his adherents have been urged, and even magnified, as if they could justify any extravagance of power to repress them. It has been asked, are these offences to pass unpunished, and are we not to vindicate our own credit, as well as that of the government, by expressing our abhorrence of them? Have I been an advocate for their passing unpunished? Have I stopped or neglected to enforce the censure of the law? Was he not prosecuted, tried and convicted, and when he left the kingdom to avoid his sentence, was he not outlawed?

Let me go farther. Had Mr. Wilkes ventured to return home whilst I had the honour to be entrusted with the executive powers of the state, he should not have remained out of custody four and twenty hours, without submitting himself to the justice or the mercy of the King, whom he had so grievously offended. He knew it, and therefore did not return till he met with more encouragement. This surely was not the behaviour, nor is this the language of one of his partizans. Compare it with the conduct of those who now hold the chief office and authority of the government, and who call so loudly for vengeance and for punishment. Did they not give their support to him abroad after his conviction and outlawry, and keep up an intercourse and correspondence with him, even whilst they were the King's ministers? Was he not permitted to return to England, to appear publicly in this capital, for months together, and to walk daily under the windows of the palace unmolested, unconfined, and unpunished? They could not plead ignorance of the seditious libel against the King and both Houses of Parliament, nor of the three impious libels contained in the Essay upon Woman, for all of which he had been legally tried and convicted.

Why then was he not called to his sentence, and the laws carried into execution, agreeable to the solemn assurances given by the King in answer to both Houses of Parliament, when they jointly addressed his majesty to carry on this prosecution? What was become of the executive power, and how were those who were invested with it justified in suspending the usual course of the law, against the express direction of the King, enforced by the recommendation of both Houses of Parliament? What were the inducements at that time to such extraordinary favour and lenity, and what are now the motives for this extraordinary resentment and severity?

The first circumstance which seems to have awakened their attention, was Mr. Wilkes offering himself a candidate for the city of London and the county of Middlesex, against the inclination of the ministry: but the proceedings against him were then carried on like the feeble efforts of men not half awake, or not half in earnest. Many days passed over before the officers of the crown would venture to execute the common process of the law for apprehending him; and to obviate this difficulty, they had at last recourse to the shameful expedient of stipulating with Mr. Wilkes himself, the terms upon which he would consent to be taken into custody. To follow that precedent you ought now at least to ask him, upon what terms he will consent to be expelled. Perhaps, if properly applied to, he may condescend to this request as graciously as he did to the former, and as voluntarily as he surrendered himself a prisoner, when he was taken with impunity out of the hands of the officers of justice by twenty persons, almost in sight of the court of King's Bench then sitting in Westminster Hall. Such was the firm and spirited conduct by which the supreme authority of the laws was supported and preserved. The outlawry was reversed for an error so trivial, that the court of King's Bench declared when they reversed it, that they were almost ashamed to mention it. When the judgment was given, the first law officer of the crown in demanding it did not think proper to enforce the penalty according to custom, and it was therefore milder than usual.

In the first session of this parliament, Mr. Wilkes was returned a member of it, and suffered to continue without any notice taken of him! The beginning of the present session passed in the same manner. What is it then which has roused the languid spirit of administration, and called down the vengeance of the House of Commons of Great Britain? Not the seditious and dangerous libel of the North Briton, not the impious libels of the Essay on Woman, not all the extravagancies which have been urged in this day's debate; all these were known before, and were not deemed sufficient for the exertion of the common censures of the law; but he has since presumed to write an insolent libel upon a secretary of state. This it seems is that capital and decisive offence, which is to raise our indignation to its highest pitch. The honour of our King, and the reverence due to our Religion, were passed over in silence and forgotten. They are now to be thrown into the scale, to make up the weight, and to induce us to espouse the quarrel of a minister.

To accomplish this important purpose, we are to violate not only the forms, but the essence of our constitution. The House of Commons is to blend the executive and judicial powers of the state with the legislative, to extend their jurisdiction, that they may take upon themselves the odium of trying and punishing in a summary manner, an offence which does not relate to themselves, but is under the immediate cognizance of the courts of law. In the exercise of it they are to form an accumulative and complicated charge, which no other court, nor even they themselves, have ever admitted in any other instance. They are to mingle up new crimes with old, and to try a man twice by the same judicature for the same offence. They are to transfer the censures of a former parliament, contrary to all precedent, and to make them the foundation of the proceedings of a subsequent one. They are to assume a power to determine upon the rights of the people, and of their representatives, by no other rule, but that of their own inclination or discretion; and, lastly, they are to attempt to persuade mankind, that they do all these things to vindicate their own honour, to express their respect for their King, and their zeal for the sacred names of their God, and their Religion.

Thus we are to add hypocrisy to violence, and artifice to oppression, not remembering, that falsehood and dissimulation are only the wrong sides of good sense and ability, which fools put on, and think they wear the robe of wisdom. If the House of Commons shall suffer themselves to be made the instrument, in such hands, to carry such a plan into execution, they will fall into the lowest state of humiliation and contempt. An individual indeed may exempt himself from the disgrace attending it, but the dishonour and odium of it will cleave to that Assembly, which ought to be the constant object of public reverence and affection. I have done my duty in endeavouring to prevent it, and am therefore careless of the consequences of it to myself.

I expect that what I have said will be misrepresented out of this House, perhaps in that place, where of all others a misrepresentation of what passes here will be most criminal. Those who have heard me must know, that I have neither invidiously aggravated, nor factiously extenuated Mr. Wilkes's offences. If he shall commit fresh crimes, they will call for fresh punishment, the law is open, that law which is the security of us all, to which Mr. Wilkes has been, and certainly will be amenable. Let him undergo the penalties of that law, whatever they may be, but not of an undefined, discretionary power, the extent of which no man knows, the extent of the mischiefs arising from it, to everything which is dear to us, no man can tell."

APPENDIX C

THE RESULT OF THE NOVEMBER ELECTIONS

THIS book was written during the early Autumn of 1926, although not finally revised until a few days after the general elections of November 2, 1926.

According to unofficial returns in the State of Pennsylvania, Mr. Vare had a majority of over 180,000. As this book goes to press, the votes are being counted in the courts of Pennsylvania, as prescribed under its laws.

No serious dispute seems to have arisen as to the election of Mr. Vare over his Democratic opponent. It is true that in certain precincts of the City of Philadelphia,—relatively few in comparison with the great number of precincts in Pennsylvania—suspicion has been aroused by the fact that Mr. Wilson, the Democratic candidate, was credited with few votes and, in a few instances, it has been proved by a recount that this was erroneous. The so-called "zero divisions" in which he is credited with no votes, may well create distrust of the result in that precinct and justify inquiry, but it does not justify any general conclusion of fraud. The strength of the inference depends upon the character of the precinct. There are precincts in Philadelphia, exclusively inhabited by citizens of the negro race, who have always voted the Republican ticket with substantial unanimity, and such fact no more justifies a conclusion that there has been fraud than a similar unanimity in behalf of a Democratic candidate in one of the white precincts of any southern state.

The author has not noticed in the press any serious contention that these mistakes of frauds are sufficient to affect the result, and if every election were invalidated because of the proof of fraud in a few election precincts, there would

125

rarely be a valid election. Therefore, I allow the statement on page 17 to stand, that the fact that Mr. Vare was elected by a substantial majority of voters of Pennsylvania will not be seriously challenged.

The same situation is true of Illinois, where Mr. Smith's plurality is, as this book goes to press, in excess of 70,000. Here again, there is no suggestion of any fraud that would affect the result.

The argument of this book is based upon the assumption that the election in either case was free from any dispute. If the right of either Senator-elect to his seat is challenged in a formal way and, upon a full and fair hearing, it develops that, in truth, the candidate was not elected, then the power of the Senate to vacate the seat, notwithstanding the temporary acceptance of his credentials, is clear.

But this right to re-judge the result of the elections, even though the authorities of the State Capitol have already determined it, must not be confused with the power to expel. The latter is a much more serious step and the framers of the Constitution believed that no such drastic punishment should be imposed upon a Senator, without the concurrence of two-thirds of the Senate. Of course, the disqualification of a Senator, on the ground that he does not possess the constitutional qualifications, is the exercise of a different power from that of expulsion.

The first instance of the exclusion of a member of Congress for lack of qualifications was the case of Albert Gallatin, elected a Senator from Pennsylvania in 1793 and excluded in 1794 for lack of the required citizenship (see *Annals of Congress,* 2d Cong., 2d Sess., Feb. 28, 1793, p. 660; *ibid,* 3d Cong., 1st Sess., Jan. 10, Feb. 11, 20, 21, 22, 24, 25, 26, 27, 28, 1794, pp. 43, 47-62). In his speech in the Senate in his own defence, Gallatin referred to the "qualifications" required by the Constitution.